北大版短期培训汉语教材

博雅速成汉语

Boya Speed-up Chinese

第一册
Book 1

李晓琪　宋绍年　刘立新　章　欣　编著
by Li Xiaoqi　Song Shaonian　Liu Lixin　Zhang Xin

北京大学出版社
PEKING UNIVERSITY PRESS

图书在版编目(CIP)数据

博雅速成汉语·第一册/李晓琪等编著. —北京：北京大学出版社，2015.2
（北大版短期培训汉语教材）

ISBN 978-7-301-25182-9

Ⅰ.①博… Ⅱ.①李… Ⅲ.①汉语—对外汉语教学—教材 Ⅳ.①H195.4

中国版本图书馆CIP数据核字(2014)第282033号

书　名	博雅速成汉语·第一册
著作责任者	李晓琪　宋绍年　刘立新　章　欣　编著
责任编辑	刘　正
标准书号	ISBN 978-7-301-25182-9
出版发行	北京大学出版社
地　址	北京市海淀区成府路205号　100871
网　址	http://www.pup.cn　新浪微博:@北京大学出版社
电子信箱	zpup@pup.pku.edu.cn
电　话	邮购部 62752015　发行部 62750672　编辑部 62753334
印刷者	北京大学印刷厂
经销者	新华书店
	720毫米×1020毫米　16开本　14.25印张　180千字
	2015年2月第1版　2015年2月第1次印刷
定　价	49.00元(含1张MP3光盘)

未经许可，不得以任何方式复制或抄袭本书之部分或全部内容。
版权所有，侵权必究
举报电话: 010-62752024　电子信箱: fd@pup.pku.edu.cn
图书如有印装质量问题，请与出版部联系，电话: 010-62756370

Foreword

前　言

　　近年来,随着汉语国际推广事业的不断发展,越来越多的外国朋友希望学习汉语,了解中国,并且希望通过短时间的学习就能顺利地到中国旅游,能与中国人谈话聊天,能和中国开展一定的贸易活动。为达此目的,我们在编写《博雅速成汉语》时以第二语言教材编写理念为指导,以方便学习者为目的,力争使之成为一套适应时代需求的新速成汉语学习教材。

　　编写第二语言学习教材,一般的做法是,口语课本多以话题情景为纲,语言知识为辅;精读课本则多以语言知识为纲,兼顾功能。前者容易忽略语言知识的系统性,后者容易忽略语言材料的实用性。本套教材努力克服上述两方面的不足,尝试把二者有机地结合起来,在以话题情景为纲组织教材内容的同时,探索功能和结构相融合的编写模式,使学习者通过学习本套教材,既掌握扎实的语言基础知识,又掌握实用的听说技能。本套教材参照《新汉语水平考试大纲》,学生学完第一册,可以达到HSK二级水平;学完第二册,可以达到HSK四级水平;学完第三册,基本可以达到HSK五级水平。

　　本套教材把日常生活用语分成了15个话题:(1)问候和介绍;(2)学校生活;(3)问路和旅游;(4)时间和日期;(5)交通;(6)在旅馆;(7)访问和做客;(8)购物;(9)季节和天气;(10)健康和医疗;(11)饮食;(12)讨论问题;(13)兴趣爱好;(14)贸易;(15)学习汉语。全套书共三册,每册15课,共计45课。每课学习一个话题的部分用语。每册为一个循环。第一册的15课是15个话题中最基本的内容,掌握了它,就可以完成简单的汉语交际。后两册在此基础上逐渐加以扩展,使每个话题得以丰富和深化。其中第三册还有意识地加入了一些商业贸易用语,以增加本书的实用性。每课设有基本句型、课文、注释、语言点、练习、生词等项目。每课的课文都包括对话,以训练听说能力;同时还设有叙述体短文,以训练阅读和理解语篇的能力。全部课文配有英文翻译。三册课文中的全部对话语体和第一册的叙述体短文标注了汉语拼音。课文和句型配有简明实用的注释,用以讲解语法知识。每课安排10个句型,20个左右生词,三册共450个句型,约900个生词。本套教材在词语和语言点的安排上注意体现重现和渐进的原则,以便于学习者学习。每课备有练习参考答案。此外,本套教材还在第一册安排了学习辅助资料,包括:语音基本知识、常用反义单音节形容词和常用俗语。

为引起学习者的兴趣,每册书后都配有三至四首古诗。

本套教材适用于在校学生的课堂教学,按照每周两课的进度,八周学完一册书。教师可以根据学习的期限和学习者的水平自由选择其中的一册(一个循环)进行教学。本套教材也可以用作会话手册,供学习汉语的各界人士自学之用。

本教材课文部分由曹莉、王舒翼女士翻译,特此致谢!

作者

2014年于北大燕园

Contents

目 录

1. 你好！ 1
   Hello!

2. 现在几点? 13
   What Time Is It?

3. 请打开书 27
   Please Open the Book

4. 银行在哪儿? 40
   Where Is the Bank?

5. 我要去北京饭店 54
   I Want to Go to Beijing Hotel

6. 我要单人房间 67
   I Want a Single Room

7. 我想去拜访您 81
   I Want to Come to Visit You

8. 一共多少钱? 95
   How Much?

9. 今天天气怎么样? 109
   How About the Weather Today?

10. 我感冒了 123
    I Have Got a Cold

11. 喝一杯绿茶吧 135
    Take a Cup of Green Tea

| 12 | 星期天你打算干什么？ | 149 |

What Are You Doing on Sunday?

| 13 | 我喜欢古典音乐 | 163 |

I Like Classical Music

| 14 | 我代表公司欢迎您 | 176 |

I Welcome You on Behalf of the Company

| 15 | 我喜欢学习中文 | 188 |

I Like Studying Chinese

生词总表 Vocabulary / 202
附录一　语法术语简称表 / 208
附录二　汉语语音 / 209
附录三　常用反义单音节形容词 / 215
附录四　常用俗语 / 216
附录五　古诗四首 / 218

1 你好!
Nǐ hǎo!
Hello!

句型 | Sentence Patterns

1. 你好!
   Nǐ hǎo!
   Hello!

2. 您好!
   Nín hǎo!
   Hello!

3. 你们好!
   Nǐmen hǎo!
   Hello! Everyone.

4. 你好吗?
   Nǐ hǎo ma?
   How are you?

5. 我很好。
   Wǒ hěn hǎo.
   I'm fine.

6. 他也很好。
Tā yě hěn hǎo.
He is fine too.

7. 我们 都很好。
Wǒmen dōu hěn hǎo.
We are all fine.

8. 你叫什么?
Nǐ jiào shénme?
What's your name?

9. 我叫 王 红。
Wǒ jiào Wáng Hóng.
I am Wang Hong.

10. 你呢?
Nǐ ne?
And you?

课文 | Text

(一)

男: 你好!
Nǐ hǎo!
Hello!

女: 您好!
Nín hǎo!
Hello, sir!

(二)

老　师: 你好吗?
Nǐ hǎo ma?
How are you?

学生A: 我很好.
Wǒ hěn hǎo.
I'm fine.

老　师: 你们好吗?
Nǐmen hǎo ma?
How are you?

学生们: 我们都很好。
Wǒmen dōu hěn hǎo.
We are all fine.

博雅速成汉语 第一册
BOYA SPEED-UP CHINESE

老　师：你叫什么？
　　　　Nǐ jiào shénme?
　　　　What's your name?

学　生：我叫王红。
　　　　Wǒ jiào Wáng Hóng.
　　　　I'm Wang Hong.

老　师：他呢？
　　　　Tā ne?
　　　　Who is he?

学　生：他叫大卫。
　　　　Tā jiào Dàwèi.
　　　　That's David.

（三）你好！Hello!

你们好，我叫王明，他叫大卫。
Nǐmen hǎo, wǒ jiào Wáng Míng, tā jiào Dàwèi.
Hello! Everyone! I'm Wang Ming. He is David.

1 你好!
Hello!

注 释 | **Annotation**

---

1. **你好！How are you? / Hello! Hi!**

    这是最常用的打招呼用语。早上、下午、晚上都可以用。

    "你好" is commonly used when greetings are exchanged. It is used in the morning, afternoon or evening.

2. **您好！How are you? / Hello! / Hi!**

    "您"是一种客气的说法，称呼长辈或尊敬的人。

    "您" is a polite form of address. It is used to address the elders or respected people.

3. **我很好。I am fine.**

    回答别人的问候"你好吗"时，要说"我很好"，不说"我好"。"很"在这里不是真的表示程度。

    When somebody greets with "你好吗", you should say "我很好" instead of "我好"."很" is not really used to express the degree or level here.

语法 | Grammar

1. 们

可以用来表示复数，如：

"们" is a plural form. For example:

（1）我———我们　　I/me—we/us
（2）你———你们　　you—you [pl.]
（3）他———他们　　he/him—they/them

2. 你好吗？

在一个句子后面加上"吗"表示疑问，这是汉语最常用的一种疑问句。如：

It is one of the most commonly used interrogative sentence in Chinese to include "吗" at the end of a sentence to express enquiry. For example:

（1）他好吗？
（2）你们好吗？

3. "也"和"都"

汉语的"也"和"都"可以出现在动词，或者副词前。例如：

In Chinese, "也" and "都" can appear before verbs and adverbs. For example:

　　(1) 他也来。　　　他们都来。
　　(2) 他也很好。　　他们都很好。

4. 他呢

　　在代词或者表示人的名词后加上"呢"，构成另一种疑问句。如：

　　It forms another type of interrogative sentence to include "呢" after pronouns or nouns which indicate people. For example:

　　(1) 我很好，你呢？
　　(2) 我叫王红，他呢？

练习 | Exercises

1. 听录音，选拼音：

Listen to the record and choose the correct pinyin:

(1) wò　　　　wǒ
(2) nǐ　　　　 nín
(3) hǎo　　　 lǎo
(4) tā　　　　 dā
(5) dōu　　　 tōu
(6) yè　　　　yě
(7) jiào　　　 qiào

（8）nǐmen　　　　nímén
（9）wómen　　　　wǒmen
（10）hèn hǎo　　　　hěn hǎo

2. 完成对话：

Complete the following dialogues:

（1）A：你好吗？
　　　B：_____，你呢？
　　　A：_____

（2）A：你们好！
　　　B：_____
　　　A：你们好吗？
　　　B：_____

（3）A：你叫什么？
　　　B：_____
　　　A：她叫什么？
　　　B：_____
　　　A：他叫什么？
　　　B：_____

3. 选择正确答案：

Choose the correct answer:

（1）A：你好！
　　　B：_____。

1 你好！ Hello!

a. 我好。   b. 您好。
c. 很好。   d. 我很好。

(2) A：你好吗？
B：_____。
a. 你好！   b. 我也很好。
c. 你们好！   d. 很好。

(3) A：你们好！
B：_____。
a. 你好！   b. 我们很好。
c. 他也很好。   d. 我们都好。

4. 连词成句：

Put the following words into sentences:

(1) 很 好 我 _____
(2) 吗 你们 好 _____
(3) 都 很好 我们 _____
(4) 很好 他 也 _____

5. 看图对话：

Talk according to the picture:

参考词语：你 好 吗 很好

生 词 | New Words

1	你	nǐ	（代）	you	你好！ How are you? / Hello! / Hi!
2	好	hǎo	（形）	fine	你好 / Hello!
3	您	nín	（代）	you (respectful form)	您好！ How are you?
4	你们	nǐmen	（代）	you (plural)	你们好！ How are you?

1 你好!
Hello!

5	吗	ma	（助）	*auxiliary word*	你好吗？ How are you? 您好吗？ How are you? 你们好吗？ How are you?
6	我	wǒ	（代）	I, me	我叫王红。 I'm Wang Hong.
7	很	hěn	（副）	very	很好/Very well. 我很好。 I'm very well.
8	他	tā	（代）	he, him	他好吗？ How's he? 他很好。 He's also very well.
9	也	yě	（副）	also, too, either	我也很好。 I'm very well, too. 他也很好。 He's also very well.
10	我们	wǒmen	（代）	we, us	我们很好。 We are all very well.
11	都	dōu	（副）	all	我们都很好。 We are all very well. 你们都好吗？ How are you all?
12	叫	jiào	（动）	to name, to be called	我叫王红。 My name is Wang Hong. 他叫大卫。 He's David.
13	什么	shénme	（代）	what	你叫什么？ What's your name? 他叫什么？ What's his name?
14	呢	ne	（助）	*auxiliary word*	我很好，你呢？ I'm very well. How about you? 我叫王红，你呢？ I'm Wang Hong, and you?

专有名词：

1	王红	Wáng Hóng	name of a person
2	大卫	Dàwèi	David
3	王明	Wáng Míng	name of a person

听力录音文本及参考答案
Recording Text and Answers

1. (1) wǒ　(2) nín　(3) hǎo　(4) tā　(5) dōu
   (6) yě　(7) jiào　(8) nǐmen　(9) wǒmen　(10) hěn hǎo
2. 略。
3. (1) b　(2) d　(3) a
4. (1) 我很好。
   (2) 你们好吗？
   (3) 我们都很好。
   (4) 他也很好。

2 现在几点?
Xiànzài jǐ diǎn?
What Time Is It?

句型 | Sentence Patterns

11. 现在几点?
Xiànzài jǐ diǎn?
What time is it now?

12. 现在 三点。
Xiànzài sān diǎn.
It is three o'clock.

13. 现在 九点 了。
Xiànzài jiǔ diǎn le.
It is already nine o'clock.

14. 银行 几点 开门?
Yínháng jǐ diǎn kāi mén?
When does the bank open?

15. 五点 十分。
Wǔ diǎn shí fēn.
Ten past five.

16. **六点半。**
Liù diǎn bàn.
Half past six.

17. **七点一刻。**
Qī diǎn yí kè.
A quarter past seven.

18. **差一刻八点。**
Chà yí kè bā diǎn.
A quarter to eight.

19. **今天是星期几?**
Jīntiān shì xīngqī jǐ?
What day is today?

20. **今天是星期日。**
Jīntiān shì xīngqīrì.
Today is Sunday.

2 现在几点？
What Time Is It?

课文 | Text

(一)

女： 大卫，现在几点？
Dàwèi, xiànzài jǐ diǎn?
David, what time is it now?

男： 现在八点。
Xiànzài bā diǎn.
It is eight o'clock.

女： 商店几点开门？
Shāngdiàn jǐ diǎn kāi mén?
When does the store open?

男： 商店八点半开门。
Shāngdiàn bā diǎn bàn kāi mén.
It opens at half past eight.

(二)

女1： 王红，几点了？
Wáng Hóng, jǐ diǎn le?
Wang Hong, what's the time?

女2： 差一刻九点。
Chà yí kè jiǔ diǎn.
A quarter to nine.

博雅速成汉语 第一册
BOYA SPEED-UP CHINESE

女1：今天是星期几？
Jīntiān shì xīngqī jǐ?
What day is today?

女2：今天是星期天。
Jīntiān shì xīngqītiān.
Today is Sunday.

女1：银行开门吗？
Yínháng kāi mén ma?
Does the bank open?

女2：银行开门。
Yínháng kāi mén.
Yes, it does.

(三)

男1：今天是星期四吗？
Jīntiān shì xīngqīsì ma?
Is it Thursday today?

男2：今天是星期三。
Jīntiān shì xīngqīsān.
No, it is Wednesday.

男1：现在几点？
Xiànzài jǐ diǎn?
What's the time now?

2 现在几点？
What Time Is It?

男2： 现在 十一点一刻。
Xiànzài shíyī diǎn yí kè.
It is a quarter past eleven now.

男1： 你说 什么？
Nǐ shuō shénme?
What did you say?

男2： 现在 是十一点十五分。
Xiànzài shì shíyī diǎn shíwǔ fēn.
It is eleven fifteen now.

注释 | Annotation

1. 今天是星期几？What day is today?

"星期"是汉语中常用的词语。从星期一到星期日依次为：

"星期" is commonly used in Chinese to express the day of the week. They are:

星期一：Monday　　星期二：Tuesday

星期三：Wednesday　星期四：Thursday

星期五：Friday　　星期六：Saturday

星期日：Sunday

2. 今天是星期天。Today is Sunday.

"星期天"也可以说成"星期日"。"星期日"多用于书面语，"星期天"多用于口语。

"星期日" is often used in written form while "星期天" is often used in oral form.

3. 差一刻九点。A quarter to nine.

在口语中，我们常常使用"一刻"的说法。"一刻"等于十五分钟。比如："十二点一刻"就是十二点十五分，"十一点

2 现在几点？
What Time Is It?

三刻"就是十一点四十五分，"差一刻十二点"就是差十五分十二点（十一点四十五分）。

"一刻", which means a quarter, is more often used in oral form. For example, "十二点一刻" is twelve o'clock and fifteen, "十一点三刻" is eleven o'clock and forty five, "差一刻十二点" is a quarter to twelve o'clock (eleven o'clock and forty five).

语法 | Grammar

1. 几

"几"用来询问数字，多用于询问十以下的数字。

"几" is used to inquire about numbers. It is more commonly used to inquire about numbers below ten.

2. 几点了？

"了"用在句子末尾，表示确定的语气。

"了" is used at the end of a sentence to express a definite mood of speaking.

3. 时间的表示 Indication of Time

5:00	五点	five o'clock
5:05	五点零五分	five past five
5:10	五点十分	ten past five
5:15	五点十五分/五点一刻	a quarter past five
5:30	五点三十分/五点半	half past five
5:45	五点四十五分/五点三刻	a quarter to six
5:55	五点五十五分/差五分六点	five minutes to six

练习 | Exercises

1. 听录音，选图片：

Listen to the record and choose the correct picture:

(1)

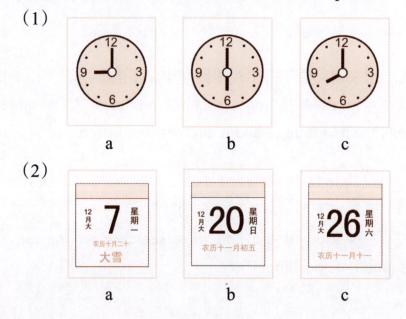

a　　　　　　b　　　　　　c

(2)

a　　　　　　b　　　　　　c

2 现在几点？
What Time Is It?

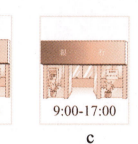

(3)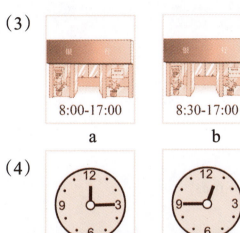

     a   b   c

(4)

     a   b   c

2. 用汉语说出下列时间：

Read the following time in Chinese:

(1) 7：00　　8：00　　11：00　　12：00
(2) 1：06　　3：14　　5：25　　8：47
(3) 1：15　　5：15　　10：45　　11：45
(4) 1：30　　4：30　　6：30　　10：30

3. 选择正确答案：

Choose the correct answer:

(1) 三点半
　　a. 2：20　b. 3：15　c. 3：30　d. 6：45
(2) 四点十四分
　　a. 4：15　b. 8：14　c. 4：40　d. 4：14

（3）五点一刻

    a. 5∶30　　　b. 5∶15　　　c. 5∶45　　　d. 5∶50

（4）差十分八点

    a. 7∶45　　　b. 8∶10　　　c. 7∶50　　　d. 8∶50

4. 完成对话：

Complete the following dialogues:

（1）A：现在几点了？

    B：_____

    A：银行开门了吗？

    B：_____

（2）A：今天是星期几？

    B：_____

5. 连词成句：

Put the following words into sentences:

（1）点　　　现在　　　八

（2）开门　　几点　　　商店

（3）商店　　开门　　　半　　　　八点

（4）是　　　星期天　　今天

（5）是　　　今天　　　吗　　　　星期四

（6）一刻　　十一　　　现在　　　点

2 现在几点？
What Time Is It?

6. 看图对话：

Talk according to the picture.

参考词语：几 点 是 吗

生词 | New Words

1	现在	xiànzài	（名）	now	你现在好吗？ How are you now? 我现在很好。 I'm very good now. 现在上课(shàng kè) Now class begins.
2	几	jǐ	（数）	how many	现在几点？ What's the time now? 几点了？ What's the time now? 几点开门？ When does it open?

3	点	diǎn	（名）	o'clock	三点 Three o'clock. 四点 Four o'clock. 现在三点。 It's three o'clock now.
4	了	le	（助）	particle	九点了 It's already nine o'clock. 几点了？ What's the time now? 开门了。 It's been open.
5	银行	yínháng	（名）	bank	银行几点开门？ When does the bank open? 银行九点开门。 The bank opens at nine o'clock. 银行开门了。 The bank's been open.
6	开	kāi	（动）	to open	开门 open the door 几点开门？ When does it open? 九点开门。 It opens at nine o'clock
7	门	mén	（名）	door	开门 open the door 八点开门。 It opens at eight o'clock. 几点开门？ When does it open?
8	分	fēn	（名）	minute	五点十分 ten past five 六点八分 eight past six 现在几点几分？ What's the time now?
9	半	bàn	（数）	half	一点半 / half past one 四点半 / half past four 现在三点半。 It's half past three now.
10	刻	kè	（量）	a quarter	一点一刻 / a quarter past one 九点三刻 / a quarter to ten 现在六点一刻。 It's one quarter past six now.

2 现在几点?
What Time Is It?

11	差	chà	(动)	short of	差十分八点 / ten to eihgt 差三分五点 / three to five 现在差十分十点。 It's ten to ten now.
12	今天	jīntiān	(名)	today	今天是星期六。 It's Saturday today. 今天银行开门吗? Does the bank open today? 今天银行开门。 The bank opens today.
13	是	shì	(动)	be, am, is, are	我是王红。 I am Wang Hong. 你是王红吗? Are you Wang Hong? 他是大卫。 He is David.
14	星期	xīngqī	(名)	week	星期一 / Monday 星期二 / Tuesday 今天是星期六。 It's Saturday today.
15	星期日(天)	xīngqīrì (tiān)	(名)	Sunday	今天是星期天。 It's Sunday today. 今天是星期日。 It's Sunday today. 今天是星期天吗? Is it Sunday today?
16	商店	shāngdiàn	(名)	shop, store	今天商店开门。 The shop is open today. 商店几点开门? When does the shop open? 商店八点开门。 The store opens at eight.

数字 0—12		
Appendix: Numbers 0—12		
零 / 0	líng	zero
一 / 1	yī	one
二 / 2	èr	two
三 / 3	sān	three

四 / 4	sì	four
五 / 5	wǔ	five
六 / 6	liù	six
七 / 7	qī	seven
八 / 8	bā	eight
九 / 9	jiǔ	nine
十 / 10	shí	ten
十一 / 11	shíyī	eleven
十二 / 12	shí'èr	twelve

听力录音文本及参考答案

Recording Text and Answers

1. （1）现在六点。
   （2）今天是星期天。
   （3）银行9点开门。
   （4）现在差一刻十二点。
   （1）b （2）b （3）c （4）c

2. 略。

3. （1）c （2）d （3）b （4）c

4. 略。

5. （1）现在八点。   （2）商店几点开门？
   （3）商店八点半开门   （4）今天是星期天。
   （5）今天是星期四吗？   （6）现在十一点一刻。

3 Qǐng dǎ kāi shū
请打开书
Please Open the Book

句型 | Sentence Patterns

21. 现在 我们 上 课。
Xiànzài wǒmen shàng kè.
Now let's begin our class.

22. 请 打开书。
Qǐng dǎkāi shū.
Please open your books.

23. 请 再说一遍。
Qǐng zài shuō yí biàn.
Please say it once again.

24. 请 读 生词。
Qǐng dú shēngcí.
Please read the new words.

25. 请 你读课文。
Qǐng nǐ dú kèwén.
Please read the text.

26. 你明白了吗？
Nǐ míngbai le ma?
Do you understand?

27. 我明白了。
Wǒ míngbai le.
I see.

28. 不，我不明白。
Bù, wǒ bù míngbai.
No, I don't understand.

29. 现在做练习。
Xiànzài zuò liànxí.
Let's do the exercises now.

30. 下课。
Xià kè.
Class is over.

3 请打开书
Please Open the Book

课文 | Text

(一)

老　师：同学们 好！
Tóngxuémen hǎo.
Hello! Everyone!

学生们：老师 好！
Lǎoshī hǎo.
Hello! Teacher!

老　师：现在 我们 上课。
Xiànzài wǒmen shàng kè.
请 打开书。
Qǐng dǎikāi shū.
Let's begin our class now. Please open your books.

同　学：老师，请您再说一遍。
Lǎoshī, qǐng nín zài shuō yí biàn.
Teacher, I beg your pardon.

老　师：请 打开书。明白了吗？
Qǐng dǎikāi shū. Míngbai le ma?
Please open the book. Do you understand?

(二)

老师： 你好，你叫什么？
Nǐ hǎo, nǐ jiào shénme?
Hello, what's your name?

同学： 我叫王红。
Wǒ jiào Wáng Hóng.
I'm Wang Hong.

老师： 他呢？
Tā ne?
Who is he?

同学： 他叫大卫。
Tā jiào Dàwèi.
He's David.

老师： 现在我们做练习。
Xiànzài wǒmen zuò liànxí.
Now let's do the exercises.

同学： 我不明白。
Wǒ bù míngbai.
Sorry, I do not understand.

老师： 我再说一次，现在做练习。
Wǒ zài shuō yí cì, xiànzài zuò liànxí.
Well, I'll repeat. Do the exercises now.

同学： 明白了。
Míngbai le.
I see.

3 请打开书
Please Open the Book

老　师：请你读课文。
　　　　Qǐng nǐ dú kèwén.
　　　　Please read the text.

同　学：好。
　　　　Hǎo.
　　　　All right.
　　　　……

老　师：现在下课。
　　　　Xiànzài xià kè.
　　　　Now the class is over.

（三）上课 Go to class

同学们好！现在我们上课。请打开书，
Tóngxuémen hǎo. Xiànzài wǒmen shàng kè. Qǐng dǎ kāi shū,
我们做练习。我再说一次，请打开书，现在读
wǒmen zuò liànxí. Wǒ zài shuō yí cì, qǐng dǎ kāi shū, xiànzài dú
生词。明白了吗？
shēngcí. Míngbai le ma?

　　Hello! Everyone! Let's begin our class now. Please open your book. let us do the exercises. I'll repeat it. Please open your book. Now read the new words. Do you understand?

注释 | Annotation

1. 同学们好！Hello everyone!

   老师称呼学生可以用"同学们"，而不用"学生们"。

   The way teachers address students is "同学们" rather than "学生们".

2. 请打开书。Please open your books.

   "请"是一个表示礼貌的用语，常常用在动词前。如：

   "请" is a word often used before the verb to give requirement politely. For example:

   (1) 请读生词。

   Please read the new words.

   (2) 请做练习。

   Please do the exercises.

语法 | Grammar

1. 请打开书。

   "打开"是一个结果补语式。动词"开"出现在"打"后，补充说明"打"的结果。

   "打开" is in the resultant complement mood. The verb "开" appears after "打" to explain the result of "打".

3 请打开书
Please Open the Book

2. 再说一遍。

动词＋"一遍",表示动作的量。其他例子如:"读一遍""做一遍"。注意,"说一次""说一遍"意思相同。

"Verb +一遍" indicates the times of the action. Other examples:"读一遍","做一遍"."说一次" has the same meaning as"说一遍".

3. 了

"了"用在动词后面,表示动作已经完成。如:

"了" is used after verbs to indicate the completion of an action. For example:

（1）他做了练习。

　　He has done the exercises.

（2）明白了吗?

　　Got it?

（3）同学们读了课文。

　　Students have read the text.

4. 不

表示否定,可以用在动词前面,也可以单独使用。

"不" express negative meaning. It can be put before verbs or used independently as well. For example:

（1）我不明白。

　　I don't understand.

（2）不，我不叫王红。
No, I am not Wang Hong.

练习 | Exercises

1. 听录音，选图片：

Listen to the record and choose the correct picture:

（1) a b c

（2) a b c

（3) a b c

3 请打开书
Please Open the Book

2. 完成对话：

Complete the following dialogues:

(1) A：同学们好！

　　B：_____

　　A：你叫什么？

　　B：我叫_____

(2) A：请你读生词。

　　B：我不明白。

　　A：请你读生词，明白了吗？

　　B：_____

3. 连词成句：

Put the following words into sentences:

(1) 吗　明白　你　了_____

(2) 一次　再　我　说_____

(3) 现在　练习　你　请　做_____

(4) 王红　了　读　生词　一遍_____

4. 用"不"将下列动词或动词词组变成否定式：

Change the following verbs or verbal phrases into negative forms with "不"：

(1) 打开书　　(2) 上课　　　(3) 读生词

(4) 读课文　　(5) 明白　　　(6) 做练习

(7) 下课　　　(8) 叫王红

5. 翻译:

Translation:

（1）现在我们上课。　　（2）我们打开了书。
（3）老师读了课文。　　（4）你说什么?
（5）我也做练习吗?　　（6）你们都做练习。
（7）我不明白你说什么。
（8）同学们请老师再读一次生词。

生词 | New Words

1	请	qǐng	（动）	please	请再说一遍。 Pardon, please. 请读生词。 Please read the new words. 请你读课文。 Please read the text.
2	打开	dǎkāi	（动）	to open	打开书 open the book 打开字典(zìdiǎn, dictionary) open the dictionary 请你打开书。 Please open the book.
3	书	shū	（名）	book	中文(Zhōngwén, Chinese)书 Chinese book 打开书 / open the book 请打开中文书。 Please open the Chinese book.
4	上课	shàng kè		to attend class	八点上课 Class begins at eight. 现在上课 Now the class begins. 你们几点上课? When do you attend your class?

3 请打开书
Please Open the Book

5	再	zài	（副）	again	再说一遍 / Please say it again. 请再读一遍 Please read it one more time. 请你再做一遍。 Please do it again.
6	说	shuō	（动）	to say	说一遍 / say it once 说中文 speak Chinese 请你说中文。 Please say it in Chinese.
7	遍	biàn	（量）	time in repetition	说一遍 / say it once 读一遍 / read it once 请再读一遍。 Please say it in Chinese.
8	读	dú	（动）	to read	读书 / read the book 读生词 / read the new words 我读中文书。 I read Chinese books.
9	生词	shēngcí	（名）	new words	一个(gè, measure word)生词 a new word 读生词 read the new words. 请你读生词。 Please read the new words.
10	课文	kèwén	（名）	text	一篇(piān, measure word)课文 / a text 读课文 / read the text 我读了一遍课文。 I've read the text once.
11	明白	míngbai	（形）	under-stand	你明白吗？ Do you understand? 他明白了。 He understands. 我们都明白了。 We've all understood.
12	不	bù	（副）	no	不好 / not good 不明白 / don't understand 他今天不上课。 He has no class to attend today.

13	做	zuò	（动）	to do	做作业(zuòyè, assignment) do homework 做练习 / do exercises 现在我们做练习。 Now let's do the exercises.
14	练习	liànxí	（名）	exercise	做练习 / do exercises 做一遍练习 do the exercises once 请你们做练习。 Please do the exercises.
15	下课	xià kè		class is over	下课了。 / Class is over. 现在下课。 Now class is over. 我们都下课了。 We all finished our classes.
16	同学们	tóngxuémen	（名）	students	同学们好。 Hello, students. 同学们做了练习。 The students have done the exercises. 请同学们读生词。 Please read the new words.
17	老师	lǎoshī	（名）	teacher	李(Lǐ, surname)老师 Mr. / Ms. 老师好。 Hello, sir / madam. 李老师好。 Hello, Mr. / Ms. Li. (teacher)
18	次	cì	（量）	once	做一次 / do it once 说一次 / say it once 请再读一次。 Please read it one more time.

听力录音文本及参考答案

Recording Text and Answers

1. （1）请打开书。

    （2）我们下课了。

    （3）A：同学们好。　　　B：老师好。

3 请打开书
Please Open the Book

    （1）a　（2）b　（3）a

2. 略。

3. （1）你明白了吗？
   （2）我再说一次。
   （3）现在请你做练习。
   （4）王红读了一遍生词。

4. （1）不打开书　　　　（2）不上课
   （3）不读生词　　　　（4）不读课文
   （5）不明白　　　　　（6）不做练习
   （7）不下课　　　　　（8）不叫王红

5. 略。

4 Yínháng zài nǎr?
银行在哪儿?
Where Is the Bank?

| 句型 | Sentence Patterns |

31. 请问，银行在哪儿？
Qǐngwèn, yínháng zài nǎr?
Excuse me, where is the bank?

32. 在前边。
Zài qiánbiān.
It is just ahead.

33. 怎么走？
Zěnme zǒu?
How can I get there?

34. 往右拐。
Wǎng yòu guǎi.
Turn to the right.

35. 银行在商店旁边。
Yínháng zài shāngdiàn pángbiān.
The bank is next to the store.

4 银行在哪儿?
Where Is the Bank?

36. 在马路左边。
Zài mǎlù zuǒbian.

It is on the left side of the road.

37. 远 吗?
Yuǎn ma?

Is it far?

38. 不远。
Bù yuǎn.

It is not far away.

39. 谢谢!
Xièxie!

Thank you!

40. 不客气。
Bú kèqi.

You're welcome.

课文 | Text

(一)

男1: 请问，银行在哪儿？
Qǐngwèn, yínháng zài nǎr?
Excuse me, Where is the bank?

男2: 银行在前边。
Yínháng zài qiánbian.
The bank is just ahead.

男1: 远吗？
Yuǎn ma?
Is it far?

男2: 不远。
Bù yuǎn.
No, it isn't.

男1: 谢谢！
Xièxie!
Thank you!

男2: 不用谢！
Bú yòng xiè.
You are welcome.

4 银行在哪儿?
Where Is the Bank?

(二)

男: 请问,商店在哪儿?
Qǐngwèn, shāngdiàn zài nǎr?

Excuse me, could you please tell me where the store is?

女: 商店在银行旁边。
Shāngdiàn zài yínháng pángbiān.

It is next to the bank.

男: 怎么走?
Zěnme zǒu?

How can I get there?

女: 往右拐。
Wǎng yòu guǎi.

Turn to the right.

男: 谢谢!
Xièxie!

Thank you!

女：不客气！
Bú kèqi.
You are welcome.

(三)

男：请问，商店在马路左边吗？
Qǐngwèn, shāngdiàn zài mǎlù zuǒbian ma?
Excuse me, is the store on the left side of the road?

女：不，商店在马路右边。
Bù, shāngdiàn zài mǎlù yòubian.
No, it is on the right side of the road.

男：银行呢？
Yínháng ne?
Then where is the bank?

女：银行也在马路右边。
Yínháng yě zài mǎlù yòubian.
The bank is also on the right side of the road.

4 银行在哪儿?
Where Is the Bank?

注释 | Annotation

1. 请问，银行在哪儿？Excuse me, where is the bank?

"请问"是一个固定格式，是汉语中最常用的礼貌用语之一，用在句子开头。

"请问", a fixed pattern, is one of the most commonly used phrases which express courtesy. It is used at the beginning of a sentence.

2. 不客气。You are welcome.

是对别人表示感谢的一种回答。也说"不用谢"。

It is a kind of reply to other people's expression of gratitude. We can also say "不用谢".

语法 | Grammar

1. 怎么走?

"怎么"用在动词"走"前,询问"走"的方向,也可以询问动作的方式。如:"怎么说""怎么读""怎么做"。

"怎么" is used before the verb "走" to express the inquiry about the direction of "走", it can also be used to ask about the way of the movement. For example:"怎么说"(how to say),"怎么"(how to read) and "怎么做"(how to do).

2. 往右拐。

"往"是一个介词,后边加上"右"组成词组"往右","往右"放在动词"拐"的前面,表示"拐"的方向。也可以说"往左拐""往南拐""往东拐"等。

"往" is a preposition followed by "右" to form a phrase "往右"."往右" is placed before the verb "拐" to indicate the direction of "拐".We can also say "往左拐","往右拐" and "往东拐" etc.

4 银行在哪儿?
Where Is the Bank?

3. 银行在哪儿?

"哪儿"是疑问代词，用来询问地点。在回答用"哪儿"提问的疑问句时，直接把信息放在"哪儿"的位置上就可以。比如：

"哪儿", a WH-word, is used to ask location. To answer the question sentence of "哪儿", just putting the information at the position of "哪儿" is okey. For example:

A：银行在哪儿?

　　Where is the bank?

B：银行在前边。

　　The bank is just ahead.

A：商店在哪儿?

　　Where the store is?

B：商店在银行左边。

　　The store is on the left side of the bank.

47

练习 | Exercises

1. 听录音，选图片：

Listen to the record and choose the correct picture:

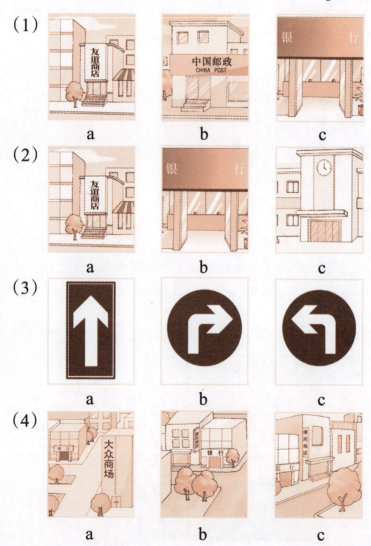

4 银行在哪儿?
Where Is the Bank?

2. 完成对话：

Complete the following dialogues:

（1）A：请问，银行在哪儿？

　　B：_____

　　A：怎么走？

　　B：_____

　　A：谢谢！

　　B：_____

（2）A：老师，商店怎么走？

　　B：_____

　　A：在马路右边吗？

　　B：_____

3. 选择合适的回答：

Choose the proper answer:

（1）A：谢谢！

　　B：_____

　　a. 谢谢！　　　b. 不用谢！　　　c. 你客气。

（2）A：谢谢！

　　B：_____

　　a. 谢谢你！　　b. 好。　　　　c. 不客气。

（3）A：请问，银行在哪儿？

　　B：_____

　　a. 不客气。　　b. 往前走。　　　c. 远。

4. 翻译：

   Translation:
   （1）在左边　　　在右边　　　在前边　　　在旁边
   （2）往右拐　　　往左拐
   （3）怎么走　　　怎么读　　　怎么说　　　怎么问

5. 选择正确的翻译：

   Choose the correct translation:
   （1）The store is next to the bank.
   　　a. 商店在旁边银行。
   　　b. 商店在银行旁边。
   　　c. 银行在商店旁边。
   　　d. 商店在银行左边。

   （2）The bank is on the right side of the road.
   　　a. 银行在马路左边。
   　　b. 银行在马路右边。
   　　c. 银行在左边马路。
   　　d. 银行在右边马路。

   （3）The store is on the right side too.
   　　a. 也商店在马路右边。
   　　b. 商店也在马路右边。
   　　c. 商店在马路也右边。
   　　d. 商店在马路右边也。

4 银行在哪儿?
Where Is the Bank?

6. 看图对话:

Talk according to the picture:

参考句式:请问,……在哪儿? 怎么走? 往……走

   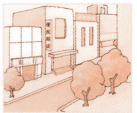

生词 | New Words

1	问	wèn	(动)	to ask, to inquire	我问你 / I ask you 他问我 / he asks me 请问,你是王红吗? Excuse me, are you Wang Hong?
2	在	zài	(动)	exist	在银行 / in the bank 在商店 / at the store 请问,银行在哪儿? Excuse me, where is the bank?
3	哪儿	nǎr	(代)	where	在哪儿 / where 银行在哪儿? Where is the bank? 王红在哪儿? Where's Wang Hong?
4	前边	qiánbian	(名)	ahead	在前边 / in front 银行在前边。 The bank is in front. 商店在前边。 The store is ahead.

5	怎么	zěnme	（代）	how	怎么走 / how to get to ... 怎么说 / how to say ... 这个生词怎么读？ How to read this new word?
6	走	zǒu	（动）	to walk	怎么走 / how to get to ... 往前边走 / walk forward 请往前边走。 Please walk forward.
7	往	wǎng	（介）	to, toward	往前走 / walk forth 往前边走 / walk forward 请往前边走。 Please walk forward.
8	右	yòu	（名）	right	右边 / right side 往右拐 / walk forward 请往右拐 / Please turn right.
9	右边	yòubian	（名）	right side	往右边拐 / turn right 银行在右边 The bank is on the right. 商店在银行右边。 The store is on the right side of the bank.
10	拐	guǎi	（动）	to turn	往右拐 / turn fight 往右边拐 / turn right 往左拐 / turn left
11	旁边	pángbiān	（名）	side	在旁边 / beside 银行在商店旁边。 The bank is beside the store. 大卫的旁边是王红。 Wang Hong is beside David.
12	马路	mǎlù	（名）	road, street	马路右边 right side of the road 银行在马路右边 The bank is on the right side of the street. 商店在马路右边 The store is on the right side of the road.

4 银行在哪儿?
Where Is the Bank?

13	左	zuǒ	(名)	left	左边 / on the left 往左拐 / turn left 银行在马路左边。 The bank's on the left side of the road.
14	左边	zuǒbian	(名)	left side	在左边 / on the left 银行在左边 The bank is on the left. 商店在银行左边。 The store is on the left side of the bank.
15	远	yuǎn	(形)	far, distant	不远 / not far 很远 / very far 商店不远。 The store is not far away.
16	谢谢	xièxie	(动)	thank you	谢谢您。/ Thank you. 谢谢你。/ Thank you. 谢谢你们。/ Thank you.
17	不用(谢)	búyòng (xiè)		You are welcome.	不用谢 / You are welcome.
18	客气	kèqi	(形)	courteous	不客气。/ You are welcome. 别(bié, don't)客气。 You are welcome. 您别客气。 You are welcome. (no need to be too courteous)

听力录音文本及参考答案
Recording Text and Answers

1. (1) 银行　(2) 商店　(3) 往右拐　(4) 银行在商店左边
   (1) c　(2) a　(3) b　(4) c

2. 略。

3. (1) b　(2) c　(3) b

4. 略。

5. (1) b　(2) b　(3) b

5 我要去北京饭店
Wǒ yào qù Běijīng Fàndiàn

I Want to Go to the Beijing Hotel

句型 | Sentence Patterns

41. 有出租车吗?
Yǒu chūzū chē ma?

Is there any taxi available?

42. 有。您去哪儿?
Yǒu. Nín qù nǎr?

Yes. Where do you want to go?

43. 您要去什么地方?
Nín yào qù shénme dìfang?

Where do you want to go?

44. 对不起,现在没有车。
Duìbùqǐ, xiànzài méiyǒu chē.

Sorry, there is no taxi available now.

45. 请等一会儿。
Qǐng děng yíhuìr.

Please wait for a moment.

5 我要去北京饭店
I Want to Go to the Beijing Hotel

46. 我要去北京饭店。
Wǒ yào qù Běijīng Fàndiàn.

I want to go to the Beijing Hotel.

47. 远不远?
Yuǎn bu yuǎn?

Is it far away?

48. 不远,一会儿就到。
Bù yuǎn, yíhuìr jiù dào.

It is not far. We will get there in a while.

49. 很远。
Hěn yuǎn.

It is so far!

50. 请上车!
Qǐng shàng chē.

Please get on the car.

课文 | Text

(一)

女: 请问, 有出租车吗?
Qǐngwèn, Yǒu chūzū chē ma?
Is there any taxi available?

男: 有, 您去哪儿?
Yǒu. Nín qù nǎr?
Yes. Where do you want to go?

女: 我去银行。去银行远不远?
Wǒ qù yínháng. Qù yínháng yuǎn bu yuǎn?
I want to go to the bank. Is it far away?

男: 不远, 一会儿就到。
Bù yuǎn, yíhuìr jiù dào.
It is not too far. We will get there in a while.

(二)

男: 您要去什么地方?
Nín yào qù shénme dìfang?
Where do you want to go?

女: 我要去北京饭店。
Wǒ yào qù Běijīng Fàndiàn.
I want to go to the Beijing Hotel.

5 我要去北京饭店
I Want to Go to the Beijing Hotel

男：请 上车。
Qǐng shàng chē.

Please get on the car.

女：谢谢！去北京饭店 远不远？
Xièxie! Qù Běijīng Fàndiàn yuǎn bu yuǎn?

Thank you! Is it far away to get to the Beijing Hotel?

男：不远，一会儿就到。
Bù yuǎn, yíhuìr jiù dào.

It is not too far. We will get there in a while.

（三）

女：请问，有没有出租车？
Qǐngwèn, yǒu méiyǒu chūzūchē?

Excuse me, Is there any taxi around?

男：对不起，现在没有车。
Duìbuqǐ, xiànzài méiyǒu chē.

Sorry, there aren't any taxis right now.

女：请再说一遍。
Qǐng zài shuō yí biàn.

I beg your pardon.

男：现在没车，请等一会儿。
Xiànzài méi chē, qǐng děng yíhuìr.

There is no taxi now. Please wait for a while.

注释 | Annotation

1. 您要去什么地方？Where do you want to go?

"什么"常常用在名词前表示询问，其他如"什么商店""什么银行""什么饭店""什么练习"。

"什么" often used before nouns to express inquiry. Other examples: "什么商店","什么银行","什么饭店" and "什么练习".

2. 对不起。Sorry.

是一种常用的、表示道歉的礼貌用语。

"对不起" is a commonly used phrase to express apologies in a courteous manner.

5 我要去北京饭店
I Want to Go to the Beijing Hotel

语法 | Grammar

1. 有

动词"有"的否定式是"没有",如果"没有"后边带有宾语,可以省略"有"。如"没有车",可以说成"没车"。

The negative form of verb "有" is "没有". If an object follows "没有", "有" can be left out. For example, "没有车" can be said as "没车"

2. 远不远

在汉语里,形容词或动词的肯定形式与否定形式连用,可以构成汉语的疑问式。其他例子如:"好不好""去不去""是不是""明白不明白"等。

The combination of the positive and negative forms of adjectives or verbs makes up another type of interrogative sentence in Chinese. Other examples: "好不好","去不去","是不是","明白不明白" etc.

3. 一会儿就到

"就"是一个副词,用在动词前,表示动作很快就会发生。例如:"我就走""他就要去机场了"。

"就" is an adverb, used before verbs to express that an act is going to take place very soon. For example:"我就走","他就要去机场了".

4. 等一会儿

动词+"一会儿",表示动作持续的时间短。其他例子如:"说一会儿""读一会儿""走一会儿"。

Verb +"一会儿" indicates that the act continues for a short time. Other examples:"说一会儿" (say for a while),"读一会儿" (read for a while) and "走一会儿" (walk for a while).

5 我要去北京饭店
I Want to Go to the Beijing Hotel

练习 | Exercises

1. 听录音，判断对错:

Listen to the record and choose whether the picture fits or not:

（1）现在没有出租车。□

（2）他要去北京饭店。□

（3）现在有出租车。□

2. 完成对话：

Complete the following dialogues:

（1）A：请问，有没有出\租车？

B：有，_____

A：我要去银行。

B：_____

A：去银行远吗？

B：不太远，_____

（2）A：今天是不是星期五？

B：不，_____

A：太好了！我们不上课。

B：_____

A：我也要去商店。

B：_____

3. 连词成句：

Put the following words into sentences:

（1）我　　　北京　　　去　　　银行　　　要

_____

（2）有　　　出租车　　　现在　　　没有　　　请问

_____

（3）对不起　　　一会儿　　　请　　　等　　　您

_____

（4）一会儿　　　到　　　不　　　就　　　远

_____

5 我要去北京饭店
I Want to Go to the Beijing Hotel

4. 选词填空：

Fill in the following blanks:

远不远　明白不明白　是不是　去不去　读不读

做不做　有没有

（1）你_____商店？

（2）银行_____八点开门？

（3）我们_____练习？

（4）北京饭店_____？

（5）同学们_____生词？

（6）王红_____书？

（7）今天_____星期天？

（8）现在没车，请等一会儿。你_____？

5. 翻译：

Translation:

（1）请上车。

（2）我读了一会儿课文。

（3）去北京饭店远不远？

（4）不远，一会儿就到。

（5）对不起，我不去银行。

生词 | New Words

1	要	yào	(动)	want	要读课文 want to read the textbook 要去北京饭店 want to go to the Beijing Hotel 他不要去银行。 He doesn't want to go to the bank.
2	去	qù	(动)	to go	去银行 / go to the bank 去商店 / go to the shop 你要去哪儿? Where are you going?
3	饭店	fàndiàn	(动)	hotel; restaurant	住饭店 / live a hotel 长城饭店 / Great Wall Hotel 在四川饭店吃晚饭 dinner at Sichuan Restaurant
4	有	yǒu	(动)	exist	前边有银行。 There's a bank in front. 银行旁边有商店。 There's a store beside the bank.
5	出租车	chūzūchē	(名)	taxi	一辆(liàng, measure word)出租车 a taxi 坐(zuò, sit)出租车 take a taxi 请问,有出租车吗? Excuse me, is there any taxi?
6	地方	dìfang	(名)	place	什么地方 / which place 你要去什么地方? Where do you want to go? 他去了什么地方? Where did he go?
7	对不起	duìbuqǐ		sorry	对不起,请再说一次。 Sorry, could you please say it again? 对不起,现在没有出租车。 Sorry, no taxi now. 对不起,我不去银行。 Sorry, I'm not going to the bank.

5 我要去北京饭店
I Want to Go to the Beijing Hotel

8	没有	méiyǒu	（动）	have not	没有出租车 / no taxi 他现在没有课。 He has no class now. 前边没有商店。 There's no store in front.
9	车	chē	（名）	car	一辆(liàng, measure word)车 a car 出租车 / taxi 现在没有车。 / No taxi now.
10	等	děng	（动）	to wait	等车 / wait for a bus/car 等出租车 / wait for a taxi 我要等他。 I want to wait for him.
11	一会儿	yíhuìr	（名）	short of	等一会儿 / wait a moment 做一会儿练习 do the exercises for a moment 请您等一会儿。 Wait a moment please.
12	就	jiù	（副）	at once; right away	一会儿就去 / go right away 我就去。 / I'll go right away. 他就要去银行了。 He is going to the bank right away.
13	到	dào	（动）	to reach	一会儿就到了 / We'll arrive soon. 我到北京饭店了。 I've arrived at Beijing Hotel. 你到哪儿了？ Where are you now?
14	上	shàng	（动）	to get on	上车 / get aboard 上出租车 / get into the taxi 请您上车。 / Get aboard please.

专有名词：

北京饭店	Běijīng Fàndiàn	Beijing Hotel

听力录音文本及参考答案
Recording Text and Answers

1. （1）A：请问，有没有出租车？
     B：有。
   （2）A：你好，我要去北京饭店。
     B：请上车。
   （3）A：现在有出租车吗？
     B：现在没车，请等一会儿。

   （1）×
   （2）√
   （3）×

2. 略。

3. （1）我要去北京银行。
   （2）请问，现在有没有出租车？
   （3）对不起，请您等一会儿。
   （4）不远，一会儿就到。

4. （1）去不去
   （2）是不是
   （3）做不做
   （4）远不远
   （5）读不读
   （6）有没有
   （7）是不是
   （8）明白不明白

5. 略。

6 Wǒ yào dānrén fángjiān
我要单人房间
I Want a Single Room

句型 | Sentence Patterns

51. 请问，有空房间吗？
Qǐngwèn, yǒu kōng fángjiān ma?

Excuse me, is there any room available?

52. 有，您要几间？
Yǒu, nín yào jǐ jiān?

Yes. How many rooms do you want?

53. 现在没有，都住满了。
Xiànzài méiyǒu, dōu zhùmǎn le.

Sorry, all rooms are full.

54. 我要两间。
Wǒ yào liǎng jiān.

I want two rooms.

55. 您要单人房间还是双人房间？
Nín yào dānrén fángjiān háishi shuāngrén fángjiān?

Do you want single room or double room?

56. 我要 双人 房间。
Wǒ yào shuāngrén fángjiān.

I want a double room.

57. 请 填 登记表。
Qǐng tián dēngjìbiǎo.

Please fill in the registration form.

58. 您的 房间是 5 0 7 号。
Nín de fángjiān shì wǔ líng qī hào.

Your room is No.507.

59. 这是 房卡。
Zhè shì fángkǎ.

This is your room card.

60. 请 跟 我 走。
Qǐng gēn wǒ zǒu.

Please follow me.

6 我要单人房间
I Want a Single Room

课文 | Text

(一)

男： 请问，有空房间吗？
Qǐngwèn, yǒu kōng fángjiān ma?
Excuse me, is there any room available?

女： 有，您要几间？
Yǒu, nín yào jǐ jiān?
Yes. How many rooms do you want?

男： 我要一间。
Wǒ yào yì jiān.
I want one room.

女： 单人房间还是双人房间？
Dānrén fángjiān háishi shuāngrén fángjiān?
A single room or double room?

男： 单人房间。
Dānrén fángjiān.
Single room.

女： 您的房间是 3 2 5 号。
Nín de fángjiān shì sān èr wǔ hào.
Your room is No. 325.

男：谢谢！
Xièxie!
Thank you!

(二)

男：请问，有没有空房间？
Qǐngwèn, yǒu méiyǒu kōng fángjiān?
Excuse me, is there any room available?

女：有双人房间，没有单人房间。
Yǒu shuāngrén fángjiān, méiyǒu dānrén fángjiān.
We have double rooms, but no single rooms.

男：好，我要双人房间。
Hǎo, Wǒ yào shuāngrén fángjiān.
Ok, I want a double room.

女：请填登记表。
Qǐng tián dēngjìbiǎo.
Please fill in the registration form.

男：好。
Hǎo.
All right.

女：这是您的房卡，请跟她走。
Zhè shì nín de fángkǎ, qǐng gēn tā zǒu.
This is your room card. Please follow her.

6 我要单人房间
I Want a Single Room

男：谢谢！
Xièxie!
Thank you!

女：不客气。
Bú kèqi.
You're welcome.

(三)

男：您要房间吗？
Nín yào fángjiān ma?
Can I help you?

女：是，我要一间单人房间。
Shì, wǒ yào yì jiān dānrén fángjiān.
Yes, I want a single room.

男：对不起，单人房间都住满了。
Duìbuqǐ, dānrén fángjiān dōu zhùmǎn le.
Sorry, we have no single rooms now.

女：有双人房间吗？
Yǒu shuāngrén fángjiān ma?
Is there any double room?

男：有。
Yǒu.
Yes.

女：好，我要一间。
Hǎo, Wǒ yào yì jiān.
OK, I want one.

男：您的房间在前边，往右拐。
Nín de fángjiān zài qiánbian, wǎng yòu guǎi.
You go ahead then turn to the right. That's your room.

女：谢谢！
Xièxie!
Thank you!

注释 | Annotation

1. 我要两间。I want two rooms.

注意，汉语的习惯说法是"两间""两点"，不说"二间""二点"。

The common saying in Chinese is "两间"，"两点" instead of "二间"，"二点".

2. 好，我要双人房间。OK, I want a double room.

"好"是个常用的应答用语，表示同意。

"好" is a phrase commonly used as an answer or a reply which indicates agreement.

语法 | Grammar

1. 都住满了。

"住满"是一个结果补语式。形容词"满"出现在"住"后,表明结果。

"住满" is in the resultant complement mood. The adjective "满" is used after "住" to show the result.

2. 单人房间还是双人房间

"还是"可构成汉语的选择问句。"还是"前后可以是名词(单人房间还是双人房间)、动词(去还是不去)、形容词(明白还是不明白),也可以是短语(你去还是我去)。

"还是" is used in an interrogative sentence to indicate a choice between two things. It can connect two nouns, verbs, adjectives or phrases. e.g. "单人房间还是双人房间" (nouns), 去还是不去 (verbs), "明白还是不明白" (adjectives), "你去还是我去" (phrase).

3. 您的房间

此处"的"是一个助词,表示领属关系。再如"我的书""他的房卡""我们的老师"。

"的" is a particle indicating the possessive relation. e.g. "我的书" (my book), "他的房卡" (his room card), "我们的老师" (our teacher).

4. 跟她走

"跟"是一个介词,后面加表示人的名词或代词,再加动词。

"跟" is a preposition, placed before pronouns or nouns which indicate people, followed by verbs.

5. 一间单人房间

"间"是个量词。汉语的数词和名词之间必须有量词,什么名词要求什么量词是确定的,如:"一本书""一辆出租汽车"。单人房间可以缩略为单人间。

"间" is a measure word. In Chinese, measure word is needed between a numeral and a noun. It is set as measure words and it should be collocated with proper nouns. such as "一本书","一辆出租汽车". 单人房间 may be abbreviated to 单人间.

6 我要单人房间
I Want a Single Room

练习 | Exercises

1. 听录音，选择合适的回答：

Listen to the record and choose the proper answer:

（1）a. 对不起。　　　b. 有，您要几间？
（2）a. 谢谢。　　　　b. 不用谢。
（3）a. 我要一间。　　b. 有双人房间吗？
（4）a. 好。　　　　　b. 不客气。

2. 用"还是"把下列各组词分别连成句子：

Make the following phrases into sentences with "还是"：

（1）你	去	商店	银行
（2）我	读	课文	生词
（3）你	要	单人房间	双人房间
（4）商店	在	马路左边	马路右边
（5）今天	是	星期六	星期天
（6）现在	商店	开门	不开门

（7）我们　　往左拐　　往右拐

_____

（8）你去　　我去

_____

3. 选择正确答案：

Choose the correct answer:

（1）A：请问，有空房间吗？

　　B：_____

　　a. 有，您要几间？　　b. 对不起，有。

　　c. 这是房卡。

（2）A：您要几间？

　　B：_____

　　a. 我要二间。　　b. 我要两间。

　　c. 我要双人房间。

（3）A：您要单人房间还是双人房间？

　　B：_____

　　a. 我要三间。　　b. 我要单人房间。　　c. 好。

（4）A：您的房间是121号，请跟我走。

　　B：_____

　　a. 不客气。　　b. 对不起。　　c. 谢谢！

6 我要单人房间
I Want a Single Room

4. 连词成句：

Put the following words into sentences:

(1) 房间　　有　　　　吗　空

_____

(2) 我　　两间　　　要　双人房间

_____

(3) 都　　单人房间　　住　了　　　满

_____

(4) 还是　您　　　　要　单人房间　双人房间

_____

(5) 登记表　请　　　填

_____

(6) 是　　这　　　房卡　您　　　的

_____

(7) 跟　　走　　　我　请

_____

5. 翻译：

Translation:

(1) 这是我的书。
(2) 我们的老师去银行了。
(3) 您的房间在前边，往左拐。
(4) 这是不是他的房卡？
(5) 对不起，我们没有空房间了。
(6) 对不起，房间都住满了。

生词 | New Words

1	单	dān	(形)	single	单人 / single person 单号 / odd numbers 有没有单人房间？ Do you have a single room?
2	人	rén	(人)	people	单人 / single (for one person) 单人房间 / single room 请问,有单人间吗？ Is there any single room available?
3	间	jiān	(量)	measure word	一间房间 / one room 有一间空房间。 There's one room available.
4	空	kōng	(形)	empty, free	空房间 / empty room 一个空房间 an empty room 有空房间吗？ Is there any rooms available?
5	房间	fángjiān	(名)	room	一个房间 / a room 没有空房间 / no room available 有几个房间？ How many rooms?
6	住	zhù	(动)	to stay	住哪儿 / where to live 住学校(xuéxiào, school) live in the school 你住在哪儿？ Where do you live?
7	满	mǎn	(形)	full	住满了 / full 没有住满 / not full 房间都住满了。 Rooms are all full.
8	两	liǎng	(数)	two	两间 / two 两次 / twice 有两个房间。 There are two rooms available.

6 我要单人房间
I Want a Single Room

9	还是	háishi	（连）	or	是学生还是老师 student or teacher 一次还是两次 / once or twice 你去商店还是去银行？ Are you going to the store or the bank?
10	双	shuāng	（形）	double	双人 / double (for two people) 双人房间 / double room 请问，有双人房间吗？ Is there any double room available?
11	填	tián	（动）	to fill	填表 / fill the blanks 填登记表 fill the registration form 请您填表。 Fill the blanks, please.
12	登记表	dēngjìbiǎo	（名）	registration form	一张(zhāng, a sheet of)登记表 a piece of registration form 填登记表 fill the registration form 请您填登记表。 Fill the registration form, please.
13	的	de	（助）	particle	我的书 / my book 我的房间 / my room 他是我的老师。 He is my teacher.
14	号	hào	（名）	number	2号 / NO. 2 单号 / odd numbers 我住416号房间。 I live in Room 416.
15	这	zhè	（代）	this	这间房间 / this room 这是我的书。 This is my book. 这是您的登记表。 This is your registration form.
16	房卡	fángkǎ	（名）	room card	你的房卡 / your room card 你有房卡吗？ Do you have your room card? 这是你的房卡。 This is your room card.

17	跟	gēn	（介）	follow	跟我走 / follow me 跟他走 / follow him 请您跟我走。 Follow me, please.
18	她	tā	（代）	she, her	她的书 / her book 她是学生。/ She is a student. 她是我的老师。 She is my teacher.

听力录音文本及参考答案

Recording Text and Answers

1. （1）请问，有空房间吗？
   （2）这是您的房卡。
   （3）对不起，单人房间都住满了。
   （4）请填登记表。
   （1）b （2）a （3）b （4）a

2. （1）你去商店还是银行？
   （2）我读课文还是生词？
   （3）你要单人房间还是双人房间？
   （4）商店在马路左边还是马路右边？
   （5）今天是星期六还是星期天？
   （6）现在商店开门还是不开门？
   （7）我们往左拐还是往右拐？
   （8）你去还是我去？

3. （1）a （2）b （3）b （4）c

4. （1）有空房间吗？
   （2）我要两间双人房间。
   （3）单人房间都住满了。
   （4）您要单人房间还是双人房间？
   （5）请填登记表。
   （6）这是您的房卡。
   （7）请跟我走。

5. 略。

7 Wǒ xiǎng qù bàifǎng nín
我想去拜访您
I Want to Come to Visit You

| 句型 | Sentence Patterns |

61. 我 想去拜访您。
Wǒ xiǎng qù bàifǎng nín.
I want to pay a visit to you.

62. 什么 时间对您合适?
Shénme shíjiān duì nín héshì?
What time will be convenient for you?

63. 您 什么时间 有空儿?
Nín shénme shíjiān yǒu kòngr?
When will you be free?

64. 星期六和星期天都 行。
Xīngqīliù hé xīngqītiān dōu xíng.
Saturdays and Sundays are all right.

65. 我 星期五 晚上 去, 可以吗?
Wǒ xīngqīwǔ wǎnshang qù, kěyǐ ma?
Can I come on Friday night?

66. 行。
Xíng.
OK.

67. 不行，我有事。
Bùxíng, wǒ yǒu shì.
Sorry, I am afraid I have got something to do.

68. 我们七点半走吧?
Wǒmen qī diǎn bàn zǒu ba?
We will go at seven thirty. Is that all right?

69. 我等你。
Wǒ děng nǐ.
I'll wait for you.

70. 再见。
Zàijiàn.
See you then.

7 我想去拜访您
I Want to Come to Visit You

课文 | Text

（一）打电话 Making a phone call

王红： 老师，您好！我是王红。
Lǎoshī, nín hǎo! Wǒ shì Wáng Hóng.
Hello, Teacher. This is Wang Hong speaking.

老师： 你好，王红。
Nǐ hǎo, Wáng Hóng.
Hello, Wang Hong.

王红： 我想去拜访您，可以吗？
Wǒ xiǎng qù bàifǎng nín, kěyǐ ma?
I want to pay a visit to you. Is that all right?

老师： 欢迎。
Huānyíng.
That's all right. You are welcome.

王红： 您什么时间有空儿？
Nín shénme shíjiān yǒu kòngr.
When will you be free?

老师： 今天下午和晚上都可以。
Jīntiān xiàwǔ hé wǎnshang dōu kěyǐ.
This afternoon and evening are both OK.

王红：我今天晚上去您家。
Wǒ jīntiān wǎnshang qù nín jiā.
I will see you tonight.

老师：可以，我等你。
Kěyǐ, wǒ děng nǐ.
All right. I will wait for you.

王红：再见！
Zàijiàn!
Goodbye!

老师：再见！
Zàijiàn!
See you then!

（二）

王红：大卫，我想去拜访老师。
Dàwèi, wǒ xiǎng qù bàifǎng lǎoshī.
David, I want to visit our teacher.

大卫：我也想去。
Wǒ yě xiǎng qù.
So do I.

王红：我们什么时间去？
Wǒmen shénme shíjiān qù?
When should we go?

7 我想去拜访您
I Want to Come to Visit You

大卫： 什么 时间对老师合适？
Shénme shíjiān duì lǎoshī héshì?

What time is appropriate for the teacher?

王红： 老师 说，晚上 她 都在家。
Lǎoshī shuō, wǎnshang tā dōu zài jiā.

The teacher says she would be at home in the evening.

大卫： 不行，晚上 我有事，我要 上课。
Bù xíng, wǎnshang wǒ yǒu shì, wǒ yào shàng kè.

But I have got something to do in the evening. I have to go to class.

王红： 星期六 晚上 呢？
Xīngqīliù wǎnshang ne?

What about Saturday night?

大卫： 星期六 晚上 可以，我没有事。
Xīngqīliù wǎnshang kěyǐ, wǒ méiyǒu shì.

Saturday night would be all right. I'm free.

王红: 我们七点半走吧?
Wǒmen qī diǎn bàn zǒu ba?
Shall we go at half past seven?

大卫: 好,我在家等你,我们一起走。
Hǎo, wǒ zài jiā děng nǐ, wǒmen yìqǐ zǒu.
All right. I will wait for you at home and then we will go together.

(三) 拜访老师 Visiting the teacher

王红和大卫想去拜访李老师,老师说
Wáng Hóng hé Dàwèi xiǎng qù bàifǎng Lǐ lǎoshī, lǎoshī shuō
晚上对她合适。今天晚上大卫要上课。
wǎnshang duì tā héshì. Jīntiān wǎnshang Dàwèi yào shàng kè.
他们想星期六晚上一起去李老师家。
Tāmen xiǎng xīngqīliù wǎnshang yìqǐ qù Lǐ lǎoshī jiā.

Wang Hong and David want to pay a visit to teacher Li. The teacher said night would be appropriate. David has to go to class this night. They want to go to visit teacher Li's home on Saturday night.

7 我想去拜访您
I Want to Come to Visit You

注释 | Annotation

1. 我想去拜访您，可以吗？I want to come to visit you. Is that all right?

在一个陈述句的后边加上"可以吗"也可以构成一种问句，表示征求对方意见。"……，行吗""……，好吗"也可以构成同类疑问句。如："你再说一遍，行吗？""我们七点半走，好吗？"

To include "可以吗" after declarative sentences can form a question which is to ask the opinions of the other party. "……，行吗？""……好吗？" can also form this kind of question. e.g. "你再说一遍，行吗？""我们七点半走，好吗？"

2. 可以，我等你。All right. I will wait for you.

"可以"可以单独回答问题，多用于书面语。"行"也可以单独回答问题，多用于口语。另外，"可以"还可以用于动词前。如："我可以去拜访您吗"

"可以" and "行" can be used to answer questions independently. "可以" is used in written form, while "行" is used in oral form. "可以" can also be used before verbs, e.g. "我可以去拜访您吗？"

语法 | Grammar

1. 什么时间对老师合适？

"对"是一个介词。作用是介绍出动作或行动的对象，如"对他很客气""对他很好""对他说"。

"对" is a preposition to introduce an act or the object of an act, e.g. "对他很客气", "对他很好", "对他说"。

2. 我们七点半走吧？

"吧"是一个语气词，用在句尾表示疑问。和"吗"不同的是，用"吧"时说话人已有基本看法，只是想证实一下。比较：今天是星期日吗？/今天是星期日吧？

"吧" is an auxiliary word that indicates mood, used at the end of sentences to express enquiry. Comparing with "吗", "吧" is used when the speaker has got a basic idea and want to make sure. Compare these two sentences: "今天是星期日吗？" / "今天是星期日吧？"

7 我想去拜访您
I Want to Come to Visit You

练习 | Exercises

1. 听录音，判断对错：

Listen to the record and judge whether the following statements are right or not:

（1）今天晚上大卫要上课。（　）
（2）他们都想去拜访老师。（　）
（3）他们十一点去银行。（　）
（4）星期天王红没有空儿。（　）

2. 读下列对话，并翻译成英文：

Read the following dialogues and translate them into English:

（1）A：王红，你有空儿吗？
　　　B：有，什么事？
　　　A：我想去银行。
　　　B：今天是星期天，银行不开门。

（2）A：我们去商店，好吗？
　　　B：好。商店远不远？
　　　A：不太远，一会儿就到。
　　　B：我和你一起去。

（3）A：你晚上有事吗？
　　　B：没事。
　　　A：我们一起去拜访老师吧？

B：可以。

（4）A：大卫，你星期天在家吗？我想去你家。

　　B：在家，欢迎你！

　　A：什么时间对你合适？

　　B：下午和晚上都可以。

3. 搭配：

Matching:

拜访　　合适
一起　　空儿
没有　　来我家
欢迎　　老师
晚上　　走

4. 把下列句子变成疑问句：

Change the following sentences into interrogative sentences:

（1）今天是星期一。

（2）现在两点。

（3）我去商店。

（4）我想下午去您家。

（5）我晚上有空儿。

（6）北京饭店不太远。

（7）我们一起去拜访老师。

7 我想去拜访您
I Want to Come to Visit You

5. 按下列要求造出疑问句：

Make interrogative sentences according to the following requirements:

(1) 用"吗"　　　　　　　(2) 用"吧"
(3) 用"呢"　　　　　　　(4) 用"还是"
(5) 用"……，可以吗"　　(6) 用"是不是"
(7) 用"有没有"　　　　　(8) 用"哪儿"
(9) 用"什么"　　　　　　(10) 用"几"

生 词 | New Words

1	想	xiǎng	（动）	to want	想去银行 want to go to the bank 不想住单人间 don't want a single room 我今天不想去北京饭店。 I don't want to go to Beijing Hotel today.
2	拜访	bàifǎng	（动）	to visit	拜访您 / visit you 拜访老师 / visit the teacher 我想今天去拜访老师。 I want to visit my teacher today.
3	时间	shíjiān	（名）	time	有时间 / have time 上课的时间 / class time 你们什么时间去？ When will you go?
4	对	duì	（介）	toward	对他说 / speak to him 对你很好 / be kind to you 我对老师说："您好！" "Hello." I said to my teacher.

5	合适	héshì	(形)	suitable	对你合适 / suitable for you 合适的时间 / suitable time 什么时间对老师合适? What time is suitable for the teacher?
6	空儿	kòngr	(名)	free	有/没有空儿 have/don't have free time 我今天没有空儿。 I'm not free today. 您什么时间有空儿? When will you be free?
7	和	hé	(连)	and	我和你 / You and I 王红和大卫 Wang Hong and David 星期五和星期六我都有空儿。 I'm free on both Friday and Saturday.
8	行	xíng	(动)	sure, all right	不行 / no 去北京饭店,行吗? What about going to the Beijing Hotel? 您住双人间,行不行? Is double room all right for you?
9	晚上	wǎnshang	(名)	night	晚上七点 seven in the evening 星期一晚上 / Monday night 晚上我没有空儿。 I'm not free at night.
10	可以	kěyǐ	(动)	can	可以去商店 can go to the store 他可以去 / He can go. 星期六我去拜访您,可以吗? Can I visit you on Saturday?
11	事	shì	(名)	matter	有事 / have something to do 没有事 / It doesn't matter. 星期三晚上你有事吗? Are you free on Wednesday night?
12	吧	ba	(助)	particle	跟我走吧? / Go with me? 我们去银行吧? Let's go to the bank? 我们十点走吧? What about leaving at ten?

7 我想去拜访您
I Want to Come to Visit You

13	再见	zàijiàn	（动）	see you then, goodbye	我去银行了,再见。I'm going to the bank. Bye-bye. 现在下课,再见。Class is over. Goodbye.
14	欢迎	huānyíng	（动）	to welcome	欢迎你 / Welcome! 北京欢迎你 Beijing welcomes you. 欢迎你到我家。Welcome to my house.
15	下午	xiàwǔ	（名）	afternoon	下午四点 / 4 p.m. 下午去商店 go to the shop in the afternoon 下午和晚上都可以。It's OK both in the afternoon and at night.
16	家	jiā	（名）	home	我家 / my home 老师家 / the teacher's home 我下午在家。I'm at home in the afternoon.
17	一起	yìqǐ	（副）	together	一起走 / go together 一起做练习 do exercises together 我们一起去老师家吧? What about going to our teacher's together?
18	他们	tāmen	（代）	they	他们是学生 / They are student 他们要去拜访李老师。They want to pay a visit to teacher Li.

听力录音文本及参考答案

Recording Text and Answers

1.（1）A：大卫,今天晚上你在家吗?

　　　B：在,你有什么事?

（2）A：星期六我要去拜访老师。

　　　B：我也想去。

（3）A：我们什么时间去银行?

　　　B：十点半吧。

（4）A：王红，星期天你有空儿吗？

　　　B：对不起，我有事。

（1）× （2）√ （3）× （4）√

2. 略。

3. 拜访老师　一起走　没有空儿　欢迎来我家　晚上合适

4.（1）今天是星期一吗？

（2）现在两点吗？

（3）你去商店吗？

（4）你想下午去我家吗？

（5）你晚上有空吗？

（6）北京饭店不太远吗？

（7）你们一起去拜访老师吗？

5. 略。

8 一共多少钱?
Yígòng duōshao qián?
How Much?

句型 | Sentence Patterns

---

71. 您要 什么?
Nín yào shénme?

May I help you?

72. 您买（一）点儿 什么?
Nín mǎi (yì) diǎnr shénme?

What do you want to buy?

73. 我要（买）十个橘子。
Wǒ yào (mǎi) shí ge júzi.

I want to buy ten oranges.

74. 还要别的吗?
Hái yào biéde ma?

Anything else?

75. 还要 两盒牛奶和一个 面包。
Hái yào liǎng hé niúnǎi hé yí ge miànbāo.

I want two boxes of milk and a loaf of bread.

76. 不要了。
Bú yào le.
No more.

77. 一共 多少 钱?
Yígòng duōshao qián?
How much?

78. 五块八毛二。
Wǔ kuài bā máo èr.
Five yuan and eighty-two.

79. 太贵了。
Tài guì le.
It is too expensive.

80. 不贵,很便宜。
Bú guì, hěn piányi.
It is not expensive. It is very cheap.

8 一共多少钱？
How Much?

课文 | Text

(一)

女：您好，您要买什么？
Nín hǎo, nín yào mǎi shénme?
Hello, may I help you?

男：我要两个面包。
Wǒ yào liǎng ge miànbāo.
I want two loaves of bread.

女：还要别的吗？
Hái yào biéde ma?
Anything else?

男：还要一盒牛奶。一共多少钱？
Hái yào yì hé niúnǎi. Yígòng duōshao qián?
And a box of milk. How much?

女：请等一下儿。一共六块三（毛）。
Qǐng děng yíxiàr. yígòng liù kuài sān (máo).
Please wait a moment. It is six yuan and thirty jiao altogether.

男：很便宜。
Hěn piányi.
It is very cheap.

女：是的，牛奶和面包都不贵。
Shì de, niúnǎi hé miànbāo dōu bú guì.
Yes, milk and bread are not too expensive.

博雅速成汉语
BOYA SPEED-UP CHINESE

(二)

女：请问，您要点儿什么？
Qǐngwèn, nín yào diǎnr shénme?
Can I help you?

男：我买橘子和苹果。
Wǒ mǎi júzi hé píngguǒ.
I want some oranges and apples.

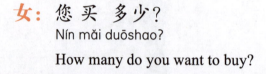

女：您买多少？
Nín mǎi duōshao?
How many do you want to buy?

男：我买五个橘子，五个苹果。
Wǒ mǎi wǔ ge júzi, wǔ ge píngguǒ.
I want to buy five oranges and five apples.

女：还要别的吗？
Hái yào biéde ma?
Anything else?

男：不要了。
Bú yào le.
No more.

女：一共三十块两毛。
Yígòng sānshí kuài liǎng máo
It is thirty yuan and twenty jiao altogether.

男： 太贵了!
Tài guì le.

It is too expensive!

(三) 去商店 Going to the store

今天是星期六，王红不上课。她要去
Jīntiān shì xīngqīliù, Wáng Hóng bú shàng kè. Tā yào qù

商店，她想买牛奶和面包。她问大卫去不去。
shāngdiàn, tā xiǎng mǎi niúnǎi hé miànbāo. Tā wèn Dàwèi qù bu qù.

Today is Sunday. Wang Hong does not have to go to class. She wants to go to the store. She wants to buy some milk and bread. She asks David if he is going too.

大卫说，他也想去商店，他要买橘子和
Dàwèi shuō, tā yě xiǎng qù shāngdiàn, tā yào mǎi júzi hé

苹果。商店8点30开门。现在差一刻九点，
píngguǒ. Shāngdiàn bā diǎn sānshí kāi mén. Xiànzài chà yí kè jiǔ diǎn,

他们一起去商店了。
tāmen yìqǐ qù shāngdiàn le.

David says he wants to go to the store too. He wants to buy some oranges and apples. The store opens at half past eight. Now it's a quarter to nine o'clock, they go to the store together.

注释 | Annotation

1. 还要别的吗？Anything else?

"别的"在这里意思是"别的东西"。"别的"常用在名词前，表示其他的，另外的，如："别的人""别的地方""别的时间""别的商店"。

"别的" is the elliptical way of saying "别的东西". "别的" is often used before nouns, e.g. "别的地方" (other places), "别的时间" (other time), "别的商店" (other stores).

2. 是的，牛奶和面包都不贵。Yes, milk and bread are not too expensive.

"是的"是个常用应答语，表示肯定。

"是的" is a common responding phrase to express the positive meaning.

语法 | Grammar

1. 一点儿

"一点儿"表示数量少,常在名词前作定语。如"买一点儿橘子""有一点儿事"。"一点儿"的"一"常常省略,如:"买点儿橘子""有点儿事"。

"一点儿" is to express a small quantity, usually used as the attributive before nouns. e.g."买一点儿橘子","有一点儿事"."一" is often left out in"一点儿", e.g."买点儿橘子""有点儿事".

2. 多少钱?

"多少"用在名词前,询问数量。如:"多少人"、"多少同学"、"多少橘子"。

"多少" is used before nouns to inquire about quantity. e.g."多少人"(how many people),"多少同学"(how many students),"多少橘子"(how many tangerines).

3. 钱数的表达 expression of monetary amounts

汉语的钱数有两种表达法,"块、毛、分"是口语形式,"元、角、分"是书面形式。最后一位的"毛"或"分"在口语中常常省去不说。如"五元八角二分""五元八角"在口语中常说成"五块八毛二""五块八"。现在,在日常生活中,"分"已经不常用了。

In Chinese there are two ways to express monetary amounts, "块、毛、分" is the oral form while "元、角、分" is the written form. The last one "毛" or "分" can be left out, e.g. "五元八角二分" and "五元八角" is often said as "五块八毛二","五块八". Nowadays, "分" is not being in use popularly.

4. 太贵了。

"太+形容词+了"是一种固定格式，表示程度很高。如"太远了""太好了""太客气了"。

"太+ adjective +了" is a fixed form to express that the degree or level is very high. e.g. "太远了" (It is too far), "太好了" (It is very good) and "太客气了" (You're too courteous).

8 一共多少钱?
How Much?

练习 | Exercises

1. 听录音,将价钱和图片连线:

Matching the prices and the pictures according to the record:

(1) 3.2元

(2) 4元

(3) 10.3元

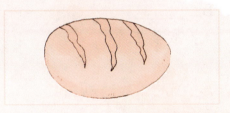

(4) 15元

2. 用汉语读出下列钱数：

Read the following monetary amounts in Chinese:

3.80元	4.07元	1.32元	45.52元
10.08元	9.40元	0.58元	21.99元

3. 完成对话：

Complete the following dialogues:

（1）　A：你要什么？

　　　B：_____

　　　A：还要别的吗？

　　　B：_____

　　　A：八块。

（2）　A：橘子好不好？

　　　B：_____

　　　A：贵吗？

　　　B：_____

　　　A：我要五个。

4. 下边哪个句子的说法正确？

Are these following sentences are correct or wrong?

（1）您什么买点儿？　　□

（2）我十个橘子要买。　□

（3）还别的要吗？　　　□

（4）一共多少钱？　　　□

（5）不贵，太便宜了。　□

8 一共多少钱?
How Much?

5. 选词填空:

Fill in the following blanks with proper word:

　　　也　　都　　还

（1）我要买面包,他（　）要买面包。
（2）单人房间和双人房间（　）住满了。
（3）今天我要去银行,（　）要去商店。
（4）你（　）去别的地方吗?
（5）你住215号,他（　）住215号,你们（　）住215号。
（6）大卫要买牛奶,（　）要面包。

6. 看图对话:

Talk according to the picture:

参考句式: 多少钱?　太……了　不贵

4元

10.3元

3.2元

15元

生词 | New Words

1	一共	yígòng	（副）	altogether	一共三个 / altogether three 一共四间 / 4 (rooms) altogether 一共十个人。/ Ten people altogether.
2	多少	duōshao	（数）	how much	多少个 / how many 今天是多少号？/ What's the date today? 你买多少个橘子？/ How many oranges do you want to buy?
3	钱	qián	（名）	money	多少钱 / how much 一共多少钱？/ How much altogether? 十个橘子一共多少钱？/ How much are ten oranges?
4	买	mǎi	（动）	to buy	买书 / buy books 买车 / buy a car 你要买什么？/ What do you want to buy?
5	一点儿	yìdiǎnr		a little	买一点儿 / buy some 您要买一点儿什么？/ What do you want to buy? 我买一点儿橘子。/ I want to buy some oranges.
6	个	gè	（量）	measure word	一个房间 / a room 六个学生 / six students 有几个房间？/ How many rooms do you have?
7	橘子	júzi	（名）	orange	一个橘子 / one orange 买橘子 / buy oranges 我想买橘子。/ I want buy some oranges.
8	还	hái	（副）	still, also	还要什么？/ What else do you want? 还买什么？/ What else do you want to buy? 我还要一个房间。/ I still want one more room.

8 一共多少钱？
How Much?

9	别的	biéde	(代)	else	别的房间 some other room 别的老师 some other teacher 您还要别的吗？ Do you want anything else?
10	盒	hé	(名)	box	一盒 / a box of 一盒牛奶 / a box of milk 我买一盒牛奶。 I buy a box of milk.
11	牛奶	niúnǎi	(名)	milk	一盒牛奶 / a box of milk 买牛奶 / buy milk 我买两盒牛奶。 I buy two boxes of milk.
12	面包	miànbāo	(名)	bread	一个面包 a loaf of bread 买面包 / buy bread 我买一个面包。 I buy a loaf of bread.
13	块(元)	kuài (yuán)	(名)	yuan	八块(元) / eight yuan 一盒牛奶四块(元)钱。 Four yuan for a box of milk. 一共三十块(元)。 Thirty yuan altogether.
14	毛(角)	máo (jiǎo)	(名)	mao (jiao)	六毛(角) / six mao 一个面包四块八毛(角)。 Four kuai and eight mao for a loaf of bread. 一共十八块八毛(角)。 Altogether eighteen kuai and eight mao.
15	太	tài	(副)	too	太好了 / very good 不太远 / not too far 桔子太贵了。 The tangerines are too expensive.
16	贵	guì	(形)	expensive	不贵 / not expensive 很贵 / very expensive 桔子太贵了。 The tangerines are too expensive.

17	便宜	piányi	（形）	cheap	很便宜 / very cheap 不便宜 / not cheap 太便宜了。/ It's so cheap.
18	一下儿	yíxiàr		a moment	问一下儿 / please ask 读一下儿 / please read 请填一下儿登记表。 Fill the registration form please.
19	苹果	píngguǒ	（名）	apple	一个苹果 / an apple 这是一个苹果 This is an apple. 我买桔子和苹果。 I want some oranges and some apples.

听力录音文本及参考答案

Recording Text and Answers

1. （1）一盒牛奶 四块

（2）六个桔子 十块三

（3）一个面包 三块二

（4）五个苹果 十五块

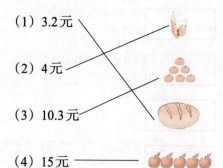

（1）3.2元

（2）4元

（3）10.3元

（4）15元

2. 略。

3. 略。

4. （1）×　（2）×　（3）×　（4）√　（5）√

5. （1）也　（2）都　（3）还　（4）还　（5）也，都　（6）也/还

9 今天天气怎么样
Jīntiān tiānqì zěnmeyàng?
How About the Weather Today?

句型 | **Sentence Patterns**

81. 今天天气怎么样?
Jīntiān tiānqì zěnmeyàng?
How about the weather today?

82. 外面 冷（热）不冷（热）?
Wàimiàn lěng (rè) bu lěng (rè)?
Is it cold (hot) out side?

83. 今天天气很好。
Jīntiān tiānqì hěn hǎo.
The weather is very good today.

84. 今天是晴天。
Jīntiān shì qíngtiān.
It is sunny today.

85. 今天是阴天，要下雨了。
Jīntiān shì yīntiān, yào xià yǔ le.
It is cloudy today. It is going to rain.

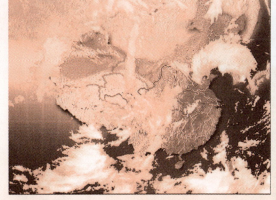

86. 外面 下雨了。
Wàimiàn xià yǔ le.
It is raining outside.

87. 刮 风了。
Guā fēng le.
The wind is blowing.

88. 风 特别大。
Fēng tèbié dà.
The wind is very strong.

89. 今天 冷极了。
Jīntiān lěng jí le.
It is extremely cold today.

90. 不 冷也不热。
Bù lěng yě bú rè.
Not too cold and not too hot.

9 今天天气怎么样?
How About the Weather Today?

课文 | Text

(一)

女: 今天天气怎么样? 外面 冷不冷?
Jīntiān tiānqì zěnmeyàng? Wàimiàn lěng bu lěng?
How about the weather today? Is it cold outside?

男: 今天是晴天,不冷也不热。
Jīntiān shì qíngtiān, bù lěng yě bú rè.
It is sunny today. Not too cold and not too hot.

女: 有风吗?
Yǒu fēng ma?
Is there any wind?

男: 没有风,天气好极了。
Méiyǒu fēng, tiānqì hǎo jí le.
There is no wind. The weather is very good.

女: 太好了! 我们一起去商店吧。
Tài hǎo le! Wǒmen yìqǐ qù shāngdiàn ba.
Great! Let's go to the store together.

男: 好。
Hǎo.
All right.

(二)

女: 外面下雨了吗?
Wàimiàn xià yǔ le ma?
Is it raining outside?

男: 是的,下雨了。
Shì de, xià yǔ le.
Yes, it is raining.

女: 雨大吗?
Yǔ dà ma?
Is it heavy?

男: 雨特别大。
Yǔ tèbié dà.
Yes, it's very heavy.

女: 也刮风了吧?
Yě guā fēng le ba?
Is the wind blowing too?

男: 也刮风了,风也特别大。
Yě guā fēng le, fēng yě tèbié dà.
Yes, and it is very strong.

9 今天天气怎么样?
How About the Weather Today?

(三) 天气不好　The weather is not good

今天天气不太好，是个阴天，要下雨了，
Jīntiān tiānqì bú tài hǎo, shì ge yīntiān, yào xià yǔ le,

也刮风了。风特别大。冷极了。
yě guā fēng le. Fēng tèbié dà. Lěng jí le.

The weather is not so good today. It is a cloudy day. The rain is coming and the wind is blowing too. The wind is very strong. It is extremely cold outside.

王红想去拜访老师，大卫说，"外面要
Wáng Hóng xiǎng qù bàifǎng lǎoshī, Dàwèi shuō: "Wàimian yào

下雨了，晚上再去吧。"王红说："好，现在
xià yǔ le, wǎnshang zài qù ba." Wáng Hóng shuō: "Hǎo, xiànzài

我们在家看书。"
wǒmen zài jiā kàn shū."

Wang Hong wants to visit her teacher. David says: "The rain is coming outside, why not go in the evening?" Wang Hong says: "All right. Let us stay at home reading now."

注释 | Annotation

1. 不冷也不热。Not too cold and not too hot.

   表示温度正好，不太冷也不太热。"不A也不B"是一个常用的格式，例如："不多也不少""不大也不小"，A、B为表示意义相反的形容词时，意思是正好，恰好，程度上正合适。

   To mean that the temperature is just good: not too cold, and also not too hot. "不A也不B" used before two adjectives opposite in meaning to indicate an intermediate state. For example, 不多也不少，不大也不小.

2. 我们一起去商店吧。Let's go to the store together.

   语气词"吧"用在句尾，除表示疑问外，也可以表示商量、请求的语气。

   An auxiliary word that indicates mood, "吧" is used at the end of a sentence, to express enquiry as well as moods of negotiation or request.

9 今天天气怎么样?
How About the Weather Today?

语法 | Grammar

1. 怎么样?

是常用的疑问词之一,用来提问。如:

"怎么样" is one of the commonly used interrogative words. For example:

你的房间怎么样?

How is your room?

这个商店怎么样?

How is the store?

你们的老师怎么样?

How is your teacher?

天气怎么样?

How is the weather?

2. 冷极了。

"形容词+极了",表示程度很高。如:

"Adjective +极了", expresses that the degree or level is very high. "极了" means to the extreme. For example:

热极了。

It is extremely hot.

远极了。

It is extremely far.

贵极了。

It is extremely expensive.

3. 要下雨了。

"要……了"表示动作将要发生。如：

"要……了" indicates that the action is going to take place or happen. For example:

要下雨了。

It is going to rain.

要刮风了。

The wind is going to blow.

要上课了。

The class is going to start.

要开门了。

The door is going to be opened.

天 气 预 报

4月12日 星期一

农历二月八

今天白天到夜间：

北京阴转晴12~18℃

风力：5-6级转4-5级

9 今天天气怎么样?
How About the Weather Today?

练习 | Exercises

1. 听录音，选图片：

Listen to the record and choose the proper picture:

(1)

(2)

(3)

(4)

2. 完成对话：
Complete the following dialogues:

（1）A：今天天气好不好？

　　B：_____

　　A：风大吗？

　　B：_____

（2）A：外面下雨了吧？

　　B：_____

　　A：冷不冷？

　　B：_____

（3）A：_____

　　B：很好，不冷也不热。

　　A：_____

　　B：没有风。

（4）A：_____

　　B：是的，外面刮风了。

　　A：_____

　　B：风大极了。

3. 把下面的词放在a、b、c、d合适的位置：
Put the word in the brackets in the proper position:

（1）a刮风b了c吧d？　　　　　　　　　　　　　　　（也）

（2）a今天是b晴天，c不冷d不热。　　　　　　　　　（也）

（3）a太好b，我们一起去c商店d吧。　　　　　　　　（了）

9 今天天气怎么样?
How About the Weather Today?

(4) 外面 a 下雨 b 了，c 晚上 d 去吧。　　　　　（再）

(5) 风 a 大 b，c 外面 d 冷极了。　　　　　　　（特别）

4. 选词填空：

Fill in the following blanks with proper word:

(1) 这个商店的苹果（　）极了。
　　a. 热　　b. 贵　　c. 远　　d. 合适

(2) 今天天气不太好，风（　）极了。
　　a. 冷　　b. 好　　c. 大　　d. 热

(3) 今天是阴天，要（　）了。
　　a. 刮风　b. 热　　c. 下雨　d. 好

5. 用线段将意义相反的词语连接起来，然后用"不……也不……"的格式造句。

Match the adversative words and then make a sentence of "不…也不…" with them.

冷　　　　　　坏
多　　　　　　少
大　　　　　　近
好　　　　　　热
远　　　　　　小

(1) 今天不冷也不热。

(2) _____

(3) _____

(4) _____
(5) _____

生词 | New Words

1	天气	tiānqì	(名)	weather	天气好 / good weather 天气不太好 bad weather 今天天气很好。 The weather is very good today.
2	怎么样	zěnmeyàng	(代)	how about	你怎么样？/ How about you? 天气怎么样？ How's the weather? 老师家怎么样？ How about the teacher's home?
3	外面	wàimiàn	(名)	outside	商店外面 / outside of the shop 外面天气怎么样？ How's the weather outside? 现在外面没有出租车。 There's no taxi outside now.
4	冷	lěng	(形)	cold	很冷 / very cold 不太冷 / not too cold 今天外面很冷。 It's very cold outside today.
5	热	rè	(形)	hot	很热 / very hot 星期五很热。 It's very hot on Friday. 外面不太热。 It's not very hot outside.
6	晴天	qíngtiān	(名)	sunny day	今天是晴天。/ It's sunny today. 星期三是晴天吗？ Will it be sunny this Wednesday? 今天天气很好，是个晴天。 It's a fine day today. It's sunny.

9 今天天气怎么样?
How About the Weather Today?

7	阴天	yīntiān	(名)	cloudy day	星期二是阴天。 Tuesday is a cloudy day. 今天天气不好,是个阴天。 It's bad weather today. It's cloudy. 今天是阴天,要下雪(xuě, snow)了。 It's cloudy today and it's going to snow.
8	要	yào	(助动)	be going to	要下雨了/It's going to rain. 我们要走了。/We are leaving. 银行要开门了。 The bank is going to open.
9	下(雨)	xià(yǔ)	(动)	to rain	下雨了。/It rains. 今天下雨吗?/Will it rain today? 要下雨了。/It's going to rain.
10	刮	guā	(动)	to blow	刮风/blow 刮大风/blow heavily 刮风了吗?/Is it blowing?
11	风	fēng	(名)	wind	没有风/no wind 风很大。 The wind blows strongly. 今天有风吗?/Is it windy today?
12	特别	tèbié	(副)	particularly	特别好/extremely good 热别热/extremely hot 外面下雨了,特别冷。 It's raining outside, and it's very cold.
13	大	dà	(形)	strong	大苹果/big apple 风特别大。/It is blowing hard. 外面的雨大吗? Is it raining heavily outside?
14	极	jí	(副)	extremely	冷极了/extremely cold 大极了/extremely big 今天是晴天,外面热极了。 It's sunny today, and it's extremely hot outside.

| 15 | 看 | kàn | (动) | look, see, watch | 看书 / read books
看电视(diànshì, television)
watch TV
让我看看。
Let me see it. |

听力录音文本及参考答案

Recording Text and Answers

1. （1）今天是晴天。
   （2）今天天气很好，不冷也不热。
   （3）外面下雨了，雨特别大。
   （4）我们在家看书吧。
   （1）a　（2）b　（3）a　（4）c

2. 略。

3. （1）a　（2）d　（3）b　（4）d　（5）a

4. （1）b　（2）c　（3）c

5. 冷——热　　多——少　　大——小
   好——坏　　远——近

10 Wǒ gǎnmào le
我感冒了
I Have Got a Cold

句型 | Sentence Patterns

91. 你身体怎么样?
Nǐ shēntǐ zěnmeyàng?
How is your health?

92. 他身体很好,什么病都没有。
Tā shēntǐ hěn hǎo, shénme bìng dōu méiyǒu.
He is very healthy. He has got no illness.

93. 他很健康。
Tā hěn jiànkāng.
He is very healthy.

94. 她身体很不错。
Tā shēntǐ hěn búcuò.
Her health is not bad.

95. 我不太舒服。
Wǒ bú tài shūfu.
I am not feeling very well.

96. 我感冒了，头很疼。
Wǒ gǎnmào le, tóu hěn téng.

I have got a flu. My head hurts badly.

97. 他病了。
Tā bìng le.

He is sick.

98. 我肚子有点儿疼。
Wǒ dùzi yǒudiǎnr téng.

I have got a slight stomachache.

99. 你应该去医院。
Nǐ yīnggāi qù yīyuàn.

You should go to the hospital.

100. 我需要休息。
Wǒ xūyào xiūxi.

I need a rest.

10 我感冒了
I Have Got a Cold

课文 | Text

(一)

男：你身体怎么样?
Nǐ shēntǐ zěnmeyàng?
How is your health?

女：我身体很好,什么病都没有。你呢?
Wǒ shēntǐ hěn hǎo, shénme bìng dōu méiyǒu. Nǐ ne?
I'm very well. I've got no illness. How about you?

男：我身体也不错。
Wǒ shēntǐ yě búcuò.
My health is not bad either.

女：外面下雨了,天气很冷。
Wàimian xià yǔ le, tiānqì hěn lěng.
It is raining outside. It is very cold.

男：是,今天特别冷。
Shì, jīntiān tèbié lěng.
Yes, it's extremely cold today.

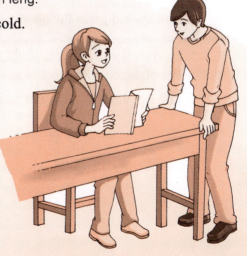

(二)

男1： 你是不是不舒服？
Nǐ shì bu shì bù shūfu?
Are you OK?

男2： 我有点儿头疼。
Wǒ yǒu diǎnr tóuténg.
I have got a slight headache.

男1： 你病了吧？今天冷极了。
Nǐ bìng le ba? Jīntiān lěng jí le.
Are you sick? Today is extremely cold.

男2： 是的，我有点儿感冒。
Shì de, wǒ yǒudiǎnr gǎnmào.
Yes, I have got a cold.

男1： 你应该去医院。
Nǐ yīnggāi qù yīyuàn.
You should go to the hospital

男2： 我不想去医院，我需要休息。
Wǒ bù xiǎng qù yīyuàn, wǒ xūyào xiūxi.
I do not want to go to the hospital. I need a rest.

10 我感冒了
I Have Got a Cold

（三） 我病了。I am sick.

我身体很健康，什么病都没有。可是今天
Wǒ shēntǐ hěn jiànkāng, shénme bìng dōu méiyǒu. Kěshì jīntiān
我有点儿不舒服，头很疼，肚子也有点儿疼。
wǒ yǒudiǎnr bù shūfu, tóu hěn téng, dùzi yě yǒudiǎnr téng.
我病了，感冒了。老师说，我应该去医院。
Wǒ bìng le, gǎnmào le. Lǎoshī shuō, wǒ yīnggāi qù yīyuàn.
我说，我不想去医院，我需要休息。
Wǒ shuō, wǒ bù xiǎng qù yīyuàn, wǒ xūyào xiūxi.

I am very healthy. I have got no illness. However, I am not feeling very well today, my head hurts badly, my stomach is aching slightly. I am sick with a flu. My teacher says, I should go to the hospital. I say, I do not want to go to the hospital. I need a rest.

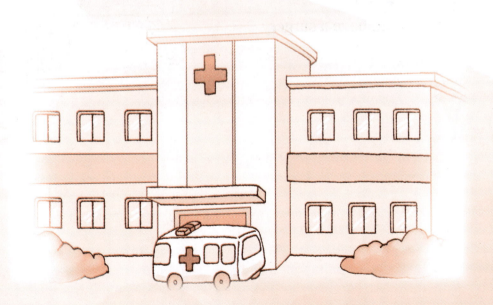

注释 | Annotation

1. 你应该去医院。 You should go to the hospital.

"应该"是一个助动词，后面要加动词或动词性词组。如：

"应该" is an auxiliary verb. It should be followed by verbs or verbal phrases. For example:

应该去商店

should go to store

应该跟我走

should follow me

应该往右拐

should turn to the right

应该动手术

should have a surgery

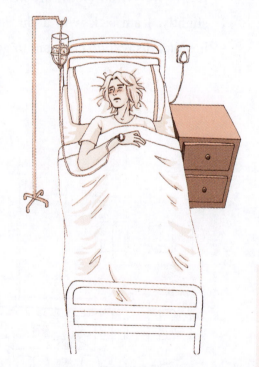

10 我感冒了
I Have Got a Cold

语法 | Grammar

1. 什么病都没有。

"什么……都"强调全部如此，没有例外。如："你什么时间来都行"。

"什么……都" emphasizes all are the same and there is no exception, e.g. "你什么时间来都行".

2. 有点儿

常用在形容词、动词前边，表示程度轻。"有点儿"也说成"有一点儿"。例如："有点儿远""有点儿贵""有一点儿疼"。

"有点儿" is often used before adjectives or verbs meaning a little, slightly. "有点儿", can also be said as "有一点儿". Examples: "有点儿远" (it is slightly far) "有点儿贵" (it is slightly expensive), "有一点儿疼" (it hurts slightly).

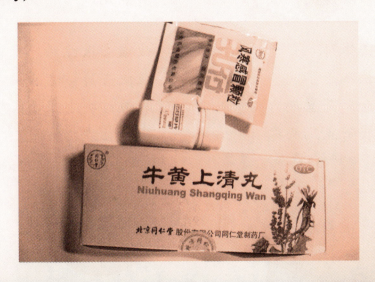

练习 | Exercises

1. 听录音，判断句子对错：

Listen to the record and judge whether the following statements are correct or not:

(1) 他身体很好。 ☐
(2) 她很健康。 ☐
(3) 现在天气很好。 ☐
(4) 我病了。 ☐
(5) 我现在在医院里。 ☐

2. 用线段连接合适的词组：

Connect the suitable phrases together:

A： 外面下雨了　　　　　　有点儿贵
　　去飞机场　　　　　　　天气有点儿冷
　　他感冒了　　　　　　　有点儿头疼
　　双人房间　　　　　　　有点儿远

B： 去银行　　　　　　　　应该去医院
　　快八点了　　　　　　　应该去拜访老师
　　今天是星期六　　　　　我应该去上课了
　　我有点儿头疼　　　　　应该往左拐

10 我感冒了
I Have Got a Cold

3. 连词成句：

Put the following words into sentences:

（1）怎么样　身体　你　_____

（2）不　我　舒服　太　_____

（3）身体　她　不错　很　_____

（4）去　你　医院　应该　_____

（5）休息　需要　我　_____

（6）他　病　什么　没有　也　_____

4. 翻译：

Translate the following sentences into Chinese:

（1）Lao Wang is very healthy. He is not sick at all.

（2）I am not feeling very well today. I do not want to go any where.

（3）Sorry, there is no room available now.

（4）I am free on Sunday. You can come at any time.

（5）He buys some books.

5. 用下面的词语写一段话：

Write a passage with the following words:

身体　健康　不舒服　感冒　头　疼　医院　需要　休息

_____

_____

_____

生词 | New Words

1	感冒	gǎnmào	（动）	flu, influenza	感冒了 / catch cold 他感冒了。/ He caught cold. 你感冒了吗？ Have you caught cold?
2	身体	shēntǐ	（名）	body	身体好 / have a healthy body 身体不好 / not healthy 我身体很好。 I'm very healthy.
3	病	bìng	（动）	to be sick	我病了。/ I'm sick. 他病了。/ He's sick. 你病了吗？/ Are you sick?
4	健康	jiànkāng	（形）	healthy	身体健康 / healthy 身体很健康 / very healthy 我的身体很健康。 I'm very healthy.
5	不错	búcuò	（形）	no too bad	身体不错 / nice body 这个商店不错。 This shop is nice. 这个房间不错。 This room is nice.
6	舒服	shūfu	（形）	comfortable, feel well	很舒服 / very comfortable 不舒服 / not comfortable 我不舒服。 I'm not feeling well.
7	头	tóu	（名）	head	头疼 / headache 头很疼 / head hurts much 我的头不疼了。 My head doesn't hurt any more.
8	疼	téng	（动）	ache, pain	头疼 / headache 肚子疼 / stomachache 我的肚子不疼了。 My stomach doesn't hurt any more.

10 我感冒了
I Have Got a Cold

9	有点儿	yǒudiǎnr	（副）	slightly, a little	有点儿贵 /a little expensive 有点儿远 / a little far 我有点儿感冒。 I've caught a slight cold.
10	肚子	dùzi	（名）	belly	肚子疼 / stomachache 肚子很疼 stomach hurts much 我的肚子有点儿疼。 My stomach slightly hurts.
11	应该	yīnggāi	（动）	should	不应该 / shouldn't 我应该去银行。 I should go to the bank. 你应该等一会儿。 You should wait a moment.
12	医院	yīyuàn	（名）	hospital	去医院 / go to the hospital 在医院 / at the hospital 你应该去医院。 You should go to the hospital.
13	需要	xūyào	（动）	need	需要钱 / need money 我需要一个老师。 I need a teacher. 你需要什么？ What do you need?
14	休息	xiūxi	（动）	rest	休息一下儿 / have a rest 休息一会儿 rest for a while 你需要休息。 You need some rest.

听力录音文本及参考答案
Recording Text and Answers

1. （1）他很健康。
   （2）她什么病也没有。
   （3）外面下雨了。
   （4）我应该去医院。

(5) 我不想去医院。
(1) √ (2) √ (3) × (4) √ (5) ×

2. A. 外面下雨了——天气有点儿冷
   去飞机场——有点儿远
   他感冒了——有点儿头疼
   双人房间——有点儿贵
   B. 去银行——应该往左拐
   快八点了——我应该去上课了
   今天是星期六——应该去拜访老师
   我有点儿头疼——应该去医院

3. (1) 你身体怎么样？
   (2) 我不太舒服。
   (3) 她身体很不错。
   (4) 你应该去医院。
   (5) 我需要休息。
   (6) 他什么病也没有。

4. 略。

5. 略。

11 喝一杯绿茶吧
Hē yì bēi lǜchá ba

Take a Cup of Green Tea

句型 | Sentence Patterns

101. 请喝茶！
Qǐng hē chá.
Please have a cup of tea.

102. 我喜欢喝啤酒。
Wǒ xǐhuan hē píjiǔ.
I like to drink beer.

103. 喝一杯绿茶吧。
Hē yì bēi lǜchá ba.
Take a cup of green tea.

104. 加一点糖吧。
Jiā yìdiǎnr táng ba.
Add a little sugar.

105. 喝茶对身体很好。
Hē chá duì shēntǐ hěn hǎo.
Drinking tea is good to health.

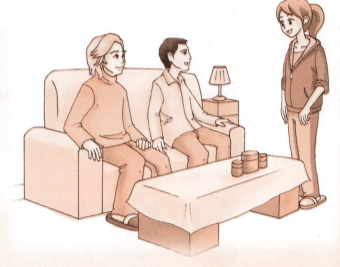

106. 要一杯咖啡,淡一点儿。
Yào yì bēi kāfēi, dàn yìdiǎnr.

I want a cup of coffee, lighter please.

107. 我喝了茶就不舒服。
Wǒ hē le chá jiù bù shūfu.

I feel uncomfortable after drinking tea.

108. 我试试。
Wǒ shìshi.

I would try.

109. 浓的、淡的我都不喜欢。
Nóng de, dàn de wǒ dōu bù xǐhuan.

I like neither thick nor light tea.

110. 花茶很香,很好喝。
Huāchá hěn xiāng, hěn hǎo hē.

Scented tea is very fragrant, and it is very nice to drink.

11 喝一杯绿茶吧
Take a Cup of Green Tea

课文 | Text

（一）请朋友喝茶 Ask friends to have some tea.

女： 你喝点儿什么？
Nǐ hē diǎnr shénme?
What would you like to drink?

男： 我喜欢喝茶。
Wǒ xǐhuan hē chá.
I like tea.

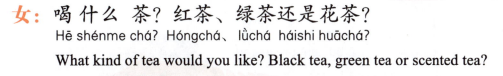

女： 喝什么茶？红茶、绿茶还是花茶？
Hē shénme chá? Hóngchá、lǜchá háishi huāchá?
What kind of tea would you like? Black tea, green tea or scented tea?

男： 喝一杯红茶吧。
Hē yì bēi hóngchá ba.
I would like a cup of black tea.

女： 喝红茶应该加糖。
Hē hóngchá yīnggāi jiā táng.
Black tea is to drink with some sugar.

男： 不，我不喜欢喝甜茶。
Bù, wǒ bù xǐhuan hē tián chá.
No, I do not like to drink with sugar.

女：牛奶呢?
Niúnǎi ne?
What about milk?

男：牛奶要一点儿。
Niúnǎi yào yìdiǎnr.
Yes, a little milk please.

(二) 在朋友家做客 To be a guest at a friend's home

女：请喝茶!
Qǐng hē chá.
Please have some tea!

男：对不起,我不喜欢喝茶。
Duìbuqǐ, wǒ bù xǐhuan hē chá.
Sorry, I do not like tea.

女：什么茶都不喜欢吗?
Shénme chá dōu bù xǐhuan ma?
Do you dislike any tea?

男：是的,我什么茶都不喝。
Shìde, wǒ shénme chá dōu bù hē.
Yes, I do not drink any tea.

女：你知道吗,喝茶对身体很好。
Nǐ zhīdào ma, hē chá duì shēntǐ hěn hǎo.
You know, drinking tea is good for your health.

11 喝一杯绿茶吧
Take a Cup of Green Tea

男: 我 知道。可是，我喝了茶就不舒服，头疼。
Wǒ zhīdào. Kěshì, wǒ hēle chá jiù bù shūfu, tóu téng.
I know. However, I would feel uncomfortable after drinking tea. My head hurts.

女: 是不是太浓了？淡一点儿就好了。
Shì bu shì tài nóng le? Dàn yìdiǎnr jiù hǎo le.
Is the tea too thick? Lighter would be better.

男: 是吗？我试试。
Shì ma? Wǒ shìshi.
Is that so? I should try some.

女: 这杯是茶，那杯是咖啡。
Zhè bēi shì chá, nà bēi shì kāfēi.
This is tea. That is coffee.

男: 谢谢，我要这杯。
Xièxiè, wǒ yào zhè bēi.
Thank you. I want this one.

（三）喝茶 Drinking tea

我 喜欢喝茶，红茶、绿茶、花茶，什么 茶
Wǒ xǐhuan hē chá, hóngchá, lǜchá, huāchá, shénme chá
都喜欢。我特别喜欢喝绿茶。绿茶很香，很好
dōu xǐhuan. Wǒ tèbié xǐhuan hē lǜchá. Lǜchá hěn xiāng, hěn hǎo
喝。我不喜欢喝咖啡，浓的、淡的、加糖的、
hē. Wǒ bù xǐhuan hē kāfēi, nóng de, dàn de, jiā táng de,
不加糖的，有牛奶的、没有牛奶的，什么咖啡
bù jiā táng de, yǒu niúnǎi de, méiyǒu niúnǎi de, shénme kāfēi

我 都 不 喝。我 喝 了 咖啡 就 不 舒服，就 头 疼。
wǒ dōu bù hē. Wǒ hē le kāfēi jiù bù shūfu, jiù tóu téng.

你 呢？喜欢 喝 什么？茶、咖啡，还是 啤酒？
Nǐ ne? Xǐhuan hē shénme? Chá, kāfēi, háishi píjiǔ?

    I like tea, any kind of tea such as black tea, green tea, and scented tea. I particularly like to drink green tea. Green tea is very fragrant and very nice to drink. I do not like to drink coffee, any kind of coffee no matter thick or light, with or without sugar, with or without milk. I would feel uncomfortable when I drink coffee. My head hurts. What about you? What do you like to drink? Do you like to drink tea, coffee or beer?

11 喝一杯绿茶吧
Take a Cup of Green Tea

注释 | Annotation

---

1. 我喜欢喝茶。I like tea.

　　茶是中国人喜欢的一种饮料，常见的有乌龙茶、绿茶和花茶。最有名的乌龙茶是铁观音，最有名的绿茶是龙井茶，最有名花茶是茉莉花茶。

　　Tea is a kind of favorite drink for Chinese. Oolong tea, green tea and scented tea are common. The most famous oolong tea is "Tieguanyin", the most famous green tea is "Longjing" and the most famous scented tea is the jasmine tea.

2. 淡一点儿就好了。Lighter would be better.

　　"一点儿"表示数量少，用在形容词后边，表示程度。如：

　　"一点儿" indicates small amount. It is used after adjectives to show the degree. For instance:

　　我希望喝淡一点儿的咖啡。

　　I want some light coffee.

　　这个菜再辣一点儿就好了。

　　This dish will be perfect if it is a little spicier.

语法 | Grammar

1. 我试试

"试试"是动词"试"的重叠式，表示动作短暂、轻松。如：

"试试" is the reduplicated form of the verb "试", indicating that the movements are brief and light. For example:

等等	wait for a while
想想	think for a while
看看	have a look

2. 浓的、淡的

"浓的、淡的"本课中意思是"浓的茶、淡的茶"。助词"的"可以加在名词、动词、形容词及各种词组后面，和前面的成分一起指代事物。如：

The meaning of "浓的", "淡的" is "浓的茶, 淡的茶". In Chinese the particle "的" can be added after nouns, verbs, adjectives and phrases to identify something. For example:

名词＋的	这杯茶是王老师的。
noun＋的	This cup of tea is the Wang's.
动词＋的	我要一点儿喝的。
verb＋的	I want something to drink.
形容词＋的	我不喜欢喝浓的。

11 喝一杯绿茶吧
Take a Cup of Green Tea

adjective + 的	I do not like drinking thick ones.
词组 + 的	加糖的
phrase + 的	those with sugar added

练习 | Exercises

1. 听录音，判断对错：

Listen to the record and judge whether the following statements are right or not:

(1)

(2)

(3)

（4）

2. 完成对话：

Complete the following dialogues:

（1）A：你要茶还是咖啡？

B：_____

A：浓一点儿的还是淡一点儿的？

B：_____

A：加糖吗？

B：不，_____

（2）A：要咖啡吗？

B：不，_____

A：你要喝什么？

B：_____

A：喝啤酒对身体不好。

B：_____

3. 连词成句：

Put the following words into sentences:

（1）糖　加　咖啡　喜欢　的　我

_____

11 喝一杯绿茶吧
Take a Cup of Green Tea

(2) 什么 茶 不 喜欢 我 都
_____

(3) 我 喝 一点儿 要 的
_____

(4) 一杯 一点儿 咖啡 淡 要 的
_____

4. 选词填空：

Fill in the following blanks with proper word:

　　　问问　试试　喝喝　读读　等等　休息休息　做做

(1) 这杯茶特别香，你（　　　）。
(2) 我要（　　　）老师，去商店怎么走。
(3) 你们（　　　）我，我一会儿就跟你们走。
(4) 你应该（　　　）喝茶，喝茶对身体有好处。
(5) 我身体不太舒服，想在家（　　　）。
(6) 外面下雨了，我什么地方也不想去，我要在家（　　）生词、（　　　）练习、（　　　）茶（　　　）。

5. 用下列词语回答问题：

Answer the questions with following words:

你喜欢喝什么饮料？它的味道怎么样？

参考词语：茶 咖啡 啤酒 浓 淡 甜 加糖 牛奶

生词 | New Words

1	喝	hē	(动)	to drink	喝牛奶 / drink milk 喝水(shuǐ, water) drink water 他喝了一盒牛奶。 He drank a box of milk.
2	杯	bēi	(名、量)	cup	绿茶 / green tea 喝绿茶 / have green tea 绿茶很好喝。 Green tea tastes very good.
3	绿	lǜ	(形)	green	喝茶 / have tea 一杯茶 / a cup of tea 喝茶对身体很好。 Tea is very good for our health.
4	茶	chá	(名)	tea	一杯花茶 a cup of scented tea 一杯啤酒 / a glass of beer 喝一杯茶吧? What about a cup of tea?
5	喜欢	xǐhuan	(动)	to like	喜欢喝茶 / like having tea 特别喜欢 / fond of 他不喜欢阴天。 He doesn't like cloudy day.
6	啤酒	píjiǔ	(名)	beer	一瓶(píng, bottle, measure word)啤酒 / a bottle of beer 喝啤酒 / drink beer 你要喝啤酒吗? Do you want some beer?
7	加	jiā	(动)	to add	加水(shuǐ, water)/ add water 加糖 / with sugar 我喝茶不喜欢加糖。 I don't like tea with sugar.
8	糖	táng	(名)	sugar	买糖 / buy sugar 吃糖 / eat sugar 我不喜欢喝加糖的咖啡。 I dislike coffee with sugar.

11 喝一杯绿茶吧
Take a Cup of Green Tea

9	咖啡	kāfēi	（名）	coffee	喝咖啡 / drink coffee 一杯咖啡 / a cup of coffee 我喝了一杯咖啡。 I had a cup of coffee.
10	淡	dàn	（形）	light	淡一点儿 / a little lighter 淡的咖啡 / light coffee 绿茶太淡了。 Green tea is too light.
11	试	shì	（动）	to try	试试 / have a try 请试一试。/ Please have a try. 不要紧，试试吧。 It doesn't matter. Just try it.
12	浓	nóng	（形）	thick	浓茶 / thick tea 浓咖啡 / thick coffee 我不喝浓茶。 I don't drink thick tea.
13	花茶	huāchá	（名）	scented tea	一杯花茶 a cup of scented tea 喝花茶 / drink scented tea 这杯花茶有点儿淡。 This cup of scented tea is a little light.
14	香	xiāng	（形）	fragrant	特别香 / very fragrant 花茶很香。 Scented tea is very fragrant. 咖啡香极了。 Coffee is very fragrant.
15	红	hóng	（形）	red	红茶 / black tea 红出租车 / red taxi 你喜欢红色吗？ Do you like red?
16.	甜	tián	（形）	sweet	甜面包 / sweet bread 糖很甜。/ Sugar is very sweet. 咖啡不太甜。 Coffee is not very sweet.
17	知道	zhīdao	（动）	to know	不知道 / don't know 我知道他感冒了。 I know he's caught a cold. 他不知道你叫什么。 He doesn't know your name.

| 18 | 那 | nà | (代) | that | 那杯咖啡 / that cup of coffee
那瓶啤酒 / that bottle of beer
我要那个房间。
I want that room. |

听力录音文本及参考答案

Recording Text and Answers

1. （1）A：你喝点儿什么？
　　　B：我喜欢喝茶。
　（2）A：喝茶对身体有好处。
　　　B：是吗？我试试。
　（3）A：你要加牛奶吗？
　　　B：不，我不喜欢加牛奶的咖啡。
　（4）A：你喜欢喝啤酒吗？
　　　B：什么啤酒我都不喝。
　（1）√　（2）√　（3）×　（4）×

2. 略。

3. （1）我喜欢加糖的咖啡。
　（2）什么茶我都不喜欢。
　（3）我要一点儿喝的。
　（4）要一杯淡一点儿的咖啡。

4. （1）试试
　（2）问问
　（3）等等
　（4）试试
　（5）休息休息
　（6）读读、做做、喝喝、休息休息

5. 略。

12 星期天你打算干什么?
Xīngqītiān nǐ dǎsuàn gàn shénme?
What Are You Doing on Sunday?

句型 | Sentence Patterns

111. 你在干什么?
Nǐ zài gàn shénme?
What are you doing?

112. 我正在看一本书。
Wǒ zhèngzài kàn yì běn shū.
I am reading a book.

113. 星期天你打算干什么?
Xīngqītiān nǐ dǎsuàn gàn shénme?
What do you plan to do on Sunday?

114. 我想去参观博物馆。
Wǒ xiǎng qù cānguān bówùguǎn.
I would like to visit the Museum.

115. 我打算去拜访一位朋友。
Wǒ dǎsuàn qù bàifǎng yí wèi péngyou.
I plan to visit a friend.

149

116. 我 先 去 商店， 然后 去看 朋友。
Wǒ xiān qù shāngdiàn, ránhòu qù kàn péngyou.

I would first go to the store, then visit my friends.

117. 那 我们一起去吧！
Nà wǒmen yìqǐ qù ba!

Then let's go together!

118. 我还 不知道做 什么。
Wǒ hái bù zhīdào zuò shénme.

I have no idea of what to do.

119. 博物馆 很有意思。
Bówùguǎn hěn yǒu yìsi.

The museum is very interesting.

120. 一点儿意思也 没有。
Yìdiǎnr yìsi yě méiyǒu.

It is not interesting at all.

12 星期天你打算干什么?
What Are You Doing on Sunday?

课文 | **Text**

(一)

男:王 红,你在干什么?
Wáng Hóng, nǐ zài gàn shénme?
Wang Hong, what are you doing?

女:我 正在看一本书。
Wǒ zhèngzài kàn yì běn shū.
I am reading a book.

男:有意思吗?
Yǒu yìsi ma?
Is it interesting?

女:不太有意思。
Bú tài yǒu yìsi.
It is not very interesting.

男:今天天气很好,我们一起去参观 博物馆吧!
Jīntiān tiānqì hěn hǎo, wǒmen yìqǐ qù cānguān bówùguǎn ba!
The weather today is very good. Let's visit the museum together!

女:好,几点走?
Hǎo, jǐ diǎn zǒu?
All right. When do we set off?

男:现在就去,怎么样?
Xiànzài jiù qù, zěnmeyàng?
Why not go now?

女：行，你等我一会儿。
Xíng, nǐ děng wǒ yíhuìr.
OK. Please wait me for a while.

（二）

女：明天是星期天，你打算做什么？
Míngtiān shì xīngqītiān, nǐ dǎsuàn zuò shénme?
Tomorrow is Sunday. What do you plan to do?

男：我要在家看书、做练习。你呢？
Wǒ yào zài jiā kàn shū, zuò liànxí. Nǐ ne?
I want to read and do some exercises at home. What about you?

女：在家一点儿意思也没有，我要出去。
Zài jiā yìdiǎnr yìsi yě méiyǒu, wǒ yào chūqu.
It is not interesting at all to stay at home. I want to go out.

12 星期天你打算干什么?
What Are You Doing on Sunday?

男: 你去什么地方?
Nǐ qù shénme dìfang?

Where do you want to go?

女: 我先去商店买一点儿橘子和苹果,然后去看一位朋友。
Wǒ xiān qù shāngdiàn mǎi yìdiǎnr júzi hé píngguǒ, ránhòu qù kàn yí wèi péngyou.

I would first go to the store to buy some oranges and apples, and then go to see a friend.

男: 我需要买牛奶和面包,我跟你一起去商店,行吗?
Wǒ xūyào mǎi niúnǎi hé miànbāo, wǒ gēn nǐ yìqǐ qù shāngdiàn, xíng ma?

I need to buy some milk and bread. Is it all right for me to go to the store with you?

女: 对不起,王红说她要和我一起去。
Duìbuqǐ, Wáng Hóng shuō tā yào hé wǒ yìqǐ qù.

Sorry, Wang Hong says she wants to go with me.

男: 那我不去了。
Nà wǒ bú qù le.

I will not go then.

（三）你星期天喜欢干什么？ What do you like to do on Sunday?

我喜欢在家，不喜欢出去。星期天我要在家喝茶，看看书，休息休息。王红呢，喜欢出去，不喜欢在家。她说在家一点儿意思也没有。星期天她要去商店，要去参观博物馆，还要去拜访朋友。大卫还不知道做什么。你星期天喜欢做什么？

Wǒ xǐhuan zài jiā, bù xǐhuan chūqù. Xīngqītiān wǒ yào zài jiā hē chá, kànkan shū, xiūxi xiūxi. Wáng Hóng ne, xǐhuan chūqù, bù xǐhuan zài jiā. Tā shuō zài jiā yìdiǎnr yìsi yě méi yǒu. Xīngqītiān tā yào qù shāngdiàn, yào qù cānguān bówùguǎn, hái yào qù bàifǎng péngyou. Dàwèi hái bù zhīdào zuò shénme. Nǐ xīngqītiān xǐhuan zuò shénme?

I like to stay at home instead of going out. I want to stay at home to drink tea, read and rest on Sunday. As to Wang Hong, she likes to go out instead of staying at home. She says it is not interesting at all to stay at home. On Sunday, she wants to go to the store, to visit the museum, and to visit friends. David does still not know what to do. What do you like to do on Sunday?

12 星期天你打算干什么?
What Are You Doing on Sunday?

注释 | Annotation

---

1. 那我们一起去吧！Let's go together!

    "那"除了有代词的意义外，还是连词，表示顺着上文的意思说出一个看法、建议。

    Other than a pronoun, "那" is a conjunction too, indicating a perspective suggestion according to the content of the prementioned message.

2. 大卫还不知道做什么。David does still not know what to do.

    "还"有两个意思，一个意思是"再"，如"我还要一杯"。另一种意思是"仍然"，如"我还不明白，请再说一遍"。

    "还" has got two meanings. One is "再", e.g. "我还要一杯" (I want another cup). The other is "仍然", e.g. "我还不明白，请再说一遍" (I still do not understand, please repeat.)

语法 | Grammar

1. 在、正在

   副词"在、正在"表示现在正在进行。如"外面正在下雨""我在喝茶"。

   "在","正在" are adverbs to express the continuous tense or the movements are still going on, e.g. "外面正在下雨" (It is raining outside), "我在喝茶" (I am drinking tea).

2. 先……然后

   这个句型表示动作发生的先后顺序。

   This sentence pattern indicates the order of the movements taking place.

3. 一点儿意思也没有。

   "一点儿……也……"是一个强调句型,强调程度很高。肯定式是"有意思"。如:

   This is an emphasis sentence pattern. The degree or level of emphasizing is very high. For this sentence, the affirmative form is "有意思". For examples:

一点钱也没有	有钱
have got no money	have got money
一点时间也没有	有时间
have got no time	have got time

12 星期天你打算干什么?
What Are You Doing on Sunday?

练习 | Exercises

1. 听录音,判断句子对错:

Listen to the record and judge whether the statement is correct or not:

(1) 我不喜欢博物馆。　　　　　　　□
(2) 我现在和朋友在一起。　　　　　□
(3) 我先去看朋友。　　　　　　　　□
(4) 我很喜欢博物馆　　　　　　　　□
(5) 很有意思。　　　　　　　　　　□

2. 填上正确的量词:

Fill in the blanks with proper measure words:

间　　位　　本　　杯　　盒　　个

一（　）朋友　　　一（　）橙汁
一（　）房间　　　一（　）牛奶
一（　）茶　　　　一（　）老师
一（　）苹果　　　一（　）书
一（　）橘子　　　一（　）银行

3. 用指定词回答问题:

Answer the questions with the given words:

(1) 你在干什么?　　　（在）
(2) 他在干什么?　　　（正在）

（3）你打算去哪儿？　　　　　　（先……，然后……）
（4）博物馆有意思吗？　　　　　（没有）
（5）我们一起去，行吗？　　　　（不，和）
（6）你现在有时间吗？　　　　　（没有）
（7）你跟他一起走吗？　　　　　（对，跟）
（8）晚上你做什么？　　　　　　（还）

4. 连词成句：

Put the following words into sentences:

(1) 在　你　什么　干

_____

(2) 看　正在　我　书　一本

_____

(3) 打算　你　星期天　什么　干

_____

(4) 去　我　想　博物馆　参观

_____

(5) 我　什么　知道　不　还　做

_____

(6) 意思　没有　一点儿　也

_____

12 星期天你打算干什么?
What Are You Doing on Sunday?

5. 用下面的词语写一段话:

Write a passage with the following words:

星期天　打算　在家　出去　先　然后　博物馆
商店　买　朋友

生词 | New Words

1	打算	dǎsuàn	(动)	to plan	打算去商店 plan to go to the bookstore 打算干什么? What's your plan? 我星期天打算去商店。 I want to go to the bookstore this Sunday.
2	干	gàn	(动)	to do	干什么 / what to do 你在干什么? What are you doing? 他们在干什么? What are they doing?

3	在	zài	(动、介)	to be; in	他们在读课文。 They are reading. 王红在买东西。 Wang Hong is shopping. 我在买橘子。 I'm buying some oranges.
4	正在	zhèngzài	(副)	in the process of	我正在买东西。 I'm shopping. 她正在买牛奶。 She is buying some milk. 你们正在干什么? What are you doing?
5	本	běn	(量)	measure word	一本书 / a book 你有几本书? How many books do you have? 我买一本书。 I buy a book.
6	参观	cānguān	(动)	to visit	去参观 / go to visit 你去哪儿参观? Which place are you going to visit? 我们在参观一个学校。 I'm visiting a school.
7	博物馆	bówùguǎn	(名)	museum	一个博物馆 / a museum 参观博物馆 visit the museum 今天我打算去博物馆。 I want to go to the museum today.
8	位	wèi	(量)	measure word	一位老师 / a teacher 两位学生 / two students 请问,你们一共有几位? Excuse me, how many guests altogether?
9	朋友	péngyou	(名)	friend	好朋友 / good friends 三个朋友 / three friends 她是我的朋友。 She is my friend.

12 星期天你打算干什么？
What Are You Doing on Sunday?

10	先	xiān	（形）	first	先买牛奶 / buy milk first 先往左拐 / turn left first 我们先干什么？ What should we do first?
11	有意思	yǒu yìsi		interesting	有意思的老师 an interesting teacher 有意思的课文 an interesting text 这本书没有意思。 This book is not interesting.
12	然后	ránhòu	（连）	then	先看生词，然后读课文 Look at new words first, and then read the text. 先去银行，然后去商店。 Go to the bank first, and then to the store. 先买桔子，然后买牛奶。 Buy tangerines first, and then buy some milk.
13	出去	chūqù	（动）	go out	不要出去。 Don't go out. 他不在家，他出去了。 He is not in. He's out. 我喜欢出去，不喜欢在家。 I like going out and dislike staying at home.
14	意思	yìsi	（名）	interest	有意思 / interesting 没有意思 / not interesting 这本书没有意思。 This book is not interesting.

听力录音文本及参考答案

Recording Text and Answers

1. （1）我想去参观博物馆。
   （2）我打算去拜访一位朋友。
   （3）我先去商店，然后去看朋友。
   （4）博物馆很有意思。

（5）一点儿意思也没有。
(1) × (2) × (3) × (4) √ (5) ×

2. 一（个/位）朋友　　　一（杯）橙汁
   一（个/间）房间　　　一（杯/盒）牛奶
   一（杯）茶　　　　　一（位/个）老师
   一（个）苹果　　　　一（本）书
   一（个）橘子　　　　一（个）银行

3. 略。

4. （1）你在干什么？
   （2）我正在看一本书。
   （3）星期天你打算干什么？/你星期天打算干什么？
   （4）我想去参观博物馆。
   （5）我还不知道做什么。
   （6）一点儿意思也没有。

5. 略。

13. 我喜欢古典音乐
Wǒ xǐhuan gǔdiǎn yīnyuè
I Like Classical Music

句型 | Sentence Patterns

121. 我很喜欢音乐。
Wǒ hěn xǐhuan yīnyuè.
I like music very much.

122. 我比较喜欢古典音乐。
Wǒ bǐjiào xǐhuan gǔdiǎn yīnyuè.
I prefer classical music.

123. 我一点儿也不喜欢流行音乐。
Wǒ yìdiǎnr yě bù xǐhuan liúxíng yīnyuè.
I do not like pop music at all.

124. 听音乐是一种享受。
Tīng yīnyuè shì yì zhǒng xiǎngshòu.
It is a kind of enjoyment to listen to music.

125. 你最爱听哪 种 音乐？
Nǐ zuì ài tīng nǎ zhǒng yīnyuè?

What kind of music do you like best?

126. 我最爱听 钢琴 曲。
Wǒ zuì ài tīng gāngqín qǔ.

I like to listen to piano tunes.

127. 你会弹 钢琴 吗？
Nǐ huì tán gāngqín ma?

Do you know how to play the piano?

128. 我 学过 弹 钢琴，可是弹得不好。
Wǒ xuéguo tán gāngqín, kěshì tán de bù hǎo.

I have learnt to play the piano, however, I do not play very well.

129. 你经 常 去听 音乐会吗？
Nǐ jīngcháng qù tīng yīnyuèhuì ma?

Do you often go to the concerts?

130. 每 个 星期六 晚上 都 去。
Měi ge xīngqīliù wǎnshang dōu qù.

I would go every Saturday evening.

13 我喜欢古典音乐
I Like Classical Music

课文 | Text

男： 你喜欢音乐吗？
Nǐ xǐhuan yīnyuè ma?
Do you like music?

女： 我很喜欢音乐。
Wǒ hěn xǐhuan yīnyuè.
I like music very much.

男： 你喜欢哪种音乐？古典音乐还是流行音乐？
Nǐ xǐhuan nǎ zhǒng yīnyuè? Gǔdiǎn yīnyuè háishi liúxíng yīnyuè?
What kind of music do you like? Classical music or pop music?

女： 我比较喜欢流行音乐。
Wǒ bǐjiào xǐhuan liúxíng yīnyuè.
I prefer pop music.

男： 我比较喜欢古典音乐。
Wǒ bǐjiào xǐhuan gǔdiǎn yīnyuè.
I like classical music better.

女： 那你经常去听音乐会吧？
Nà nǐ jīngcháng qù tīng yīnyuèhuì ba?
Do you often go to the concerts?

男： 是，每个星期六晚上都去。
Shì, měi ge xīngqīliù wǎnshang dōu qù.
Yes, I would go every Saturday night.

(二)

女： 你最爱听哪种音乐？
Nǐ zuì ài tīng nǎ zhǒng yīnyuè?
What kind of music do you like best?

男： 我最爱听钢琴曲。
Wǒ zuì ài tīng gāngqínqǔ.
I love listening to piano tunes.

女： 我也喜欢听钢琴曲，那是一种享受。
Wǒ yě xǐhuan tīng gāngqínqǔ, nà shì yì zhǒng xiǎngshòu.
I like to listen to piano tunes too. That is a kind of enjoyment.

男： 你会弹钢琴吗？
Nǐ huì tán gāngqín ma?
Do you know how to play the piano?

女： 不，我一点儿也不会弹。你呢？
Bù, wǒ yìdiǎnr yě bú huì tán. Nǐ ne?
No, I can not at all. What about you?

男： 我会一点儿，我学过弹钢琴，可是弹得不好。
Wǒ huì yìdiǎnr, wǒ xuéguo tán gāngqín, kěshì tán de bù hǎo.
I can play a little. I have learnt to play the piano. However, I do not play very well.

13 我喜欢古典音乐
I Like Classical Music

（三）我同意了 I agree

我和大卫都喜欢音乐。今天是星期六，我们没有别的事，打算一起去听音乐会。可是大卫喜欢流行音乐，不喜欢古典音乐。我呢，一点儿也不喜欢流行音乐，我喜欢古典音乐。我们不知道应该去哪个音乐会。大卫说，听音乐是一种享受，听不喜欢的音乐没意思，我们不要一起去了！我同意了。

Wǒ hé Dàwèi dōu xǐhuan yīnyuè. Jīntiān shì xīngqīliù, wǒmen méiyǒu biéde shì, dǎsuàn yìqǐ qù tīng yīnyuèhuì. Kěshì Dàwèi xǐhuan liúxíng yīnyuè, bù xǐhuan gǔdiǎn yīnyuè. Wǒ ne, yìdiǎnr yě bù xǐhuan liúxíng yīnyuè, wǒ xǐhuan gǔdiǎn yīnyuè. Wǒmen bù zhīdào yīnggāi qù nǎ ge yīnyuèhuì. Dàwèi shuō, tīng yīnyuè shì yì zhǒng xiǎngshòu, tīng bù xǐhuan de yīnyuè méi yìsi, wǒmen búyào yìqǐ qù le! Wǒ tóngyì le.

Both David and I like music. Today is Saturday. We have got nothing special on, so we plan to go to the concert together. However, David likes pop music. He does not like classical music. As for me, I do not like pop music at all. I like classical music. We do not know which concert to go to. David says, Listening to music is a kind of enjoyment. Listening to music which one does not like would be meaningless, so we should not go together! I agree with him.

注释 | Annotation

1. 那是一种享受。That is a kind of treat.

    "种"是"享受"的量词,表示一类事物,如"音乐""茶"等。

    "种" is the measure word of "享受", it indicate one kind of things. Such as "音乐" and "茶".

2. 我一点儿也不会弹。I can not play at all.

    这句话的意思是"我完全不会弹"。"一点儿也不"意思是"完全不"

    The meaning of this sentence is "I entirely can not play (piano)".

13 我喜欢古典音乐
I Like Classical Music

语法 | Grammar

1. 每个星期六晚上都去。

"每……都……"常在一起用，强调没有例外。如：

"每……都……" is often used together, emphasizing that no exception is allowed. For examples:

他每天都喝绿茶。

He drinks green tea everyday.

我每个月都去银行。

I go to the bank every month.

每次去商店，他都买水果。

He buys fruit every time he goes to the store.

2. 我学过弹钢琴。

"过"是一个动态助词，放在动词后表示有某种经历。如：

"过" is an aspectual particle, which is placed after verbs to express the experience, like past tense or perfect tense. For examples:

（我）去过飞机场

(I have) been to the airport.

（他）听过音乐会

(He has) been to the concert.

（他们）拜访过老师

(They have) visited the teacher.

3. 弹得不好。

结构助词"得"后的成分补充说明前边的动词怎么样。肯定式有"弹得好""弹得比较好""弹得特别好"等。

The elements after the structural particle "得" further illustrate how the verb is used. The affirmative forms are: "弹得好" (play well), "弹得比较好" (play better), "弹得特别好" (play the best) etc.

练习 | Exercises

1. 听录音,判断对错:

Listen to the record and judge whether the statements are correct or not:

(1) 男的喜欢听音乐会。　□
(2) 女的一点儿也不会弹钢琴。　□
(3) 他们一起去听音乐会了。　□
(4) 他们都喜欢听音乐。　□

13 我喜欢古典音乐
I Like Classical Music

2. 完成对话：

Complete the following dialogues:

（1） A：晚上你打算干什么？

　　 B：_____

　　 A：你喜欢听哪种音乐？

　　 B：_____

　　 A：你经常听音乐会吗？

　　 B：_____

（2） A：你会弹钢琴吗？

　　 B：_____

　　 A：你的钢琴弹得怎么样？

　　 B：_____。你呢？

　　 A：我不会弹钢琴，我没学过。

3. 翻译：

Translation:

（1） I love listening to classical music.

（2） He plays the piano extremely well.

（3） All of us visit the museum every Sunday.

（4） I have read every book.

（5） Every teacher likes to drink tea.

（6） Have you been to the airport?

（7） Have you visited the Art Museum?

4. 把下面的句子按正确的顺序排列：

Fill in the following blanks with proper word:

（1）他们不知道应该去哪个音乐会。

（2）星期天晚上，他们打算一起去听音乐会。

（3）可是，王红喜欢流行音乐。

（4）王红和大卫都喜欢音乐。

（5）大卫喜欢古典音乐。

5. 用下列词语说一段话：

Make a speech with the following words:

参考词语：喜欢　古典　流行　音乐
　　　　　钢琴　经常　音乐会

生词 | New Words

1	古典	gǔdiǎn	（名）	classical	古典音乐 / classical music 古典小说(xiǎoshuō, novel) 我喜欢古典音乐。 I like classical music.
2	音乐	yīnyuè	（名）	music	音乐会 / concert 喜欢音乐 love music 你喜欢什么音乐？ What kind of music do you like?

13 我喜欢古典音乐
I Like Classical Music

3	比较	bǐjiào	(副)	rather	比较冷 / rather cold 银行比较远。 The bank is quite far. 我比较喜欢喝咖啡。 I prefer coffee.
4	流行	liúxíng	(形)	popular	流行音乐 / pop music 比较流行 / quite popular 你喜欢流行音乐吗? Do you like pop music?
5	听	tīng	(动)	to listen	听音乐 / listen to the music 听音乐会 / enjoy a concert 我听他读课文。 I listened to him reading the book.
6	种	zhǒng	(量)	kind, type	一种音乐 / a type of music 这种苹果 / this kind of apple 你喝过这种茶吗? Have you ever had this kind of tea?
7	享受	xiǎngshòu	(动、名)	to enjoy (ment)	享受生活(shēnghuó, life) enjoy the life 享受音乐 / enjoy the music 听音乐是一种享受。 Music is a kind of enjoyment.
8	最	zuì	(副)	most, best	最大 / the biggest 最流行 / the most popular 我最喜欢流行音乐。 I like pop music most.
9	爱	ài	(动)	to love	爱音乐 / love music 爱喝咖啡 / love having coffee 我爱听古典音乐。 I love classical music.
10	哪	nǎ	(代)	which	哪个人 / which person 哪种音乐 / which kind of music 哪杯是咖啡? Which cup is coffee?

11	钢琴	gāngqín	(名)	piano	一架(jià, measure word)钢琴 a piano 弹钢琴 / play the piano 你家有钢琴吗? Do you have a piano at home?
12	曲	qǔ	(名)	tune	钢琴曲 / piano tune 一首(shǒu, measure word)钢琴曲 / a piano tune 这是我最喜欢的钢琴曲。 This is my favorite piano tune.
13	会	huì	(动)	to know	会弹钢琴 / can play the piano 会说中文 can speak Chinese 我一点儿中文也不会说。 I can't speak any Chinese.
14	弹	tán	(动)	to play	弹钢琴 / play the piano 弹吉他(jítā, guitar) play the guitar 你会弹钢琴吗? Can you play the piano?
15	学	xué	(动)	to learn	学弹钢琴 / learn to play the piano 学生词 / learn new words 我正在学中文 I'm learning Chinese.
16	过	guo	(助)	particle	读过课文 / have read the text 没有喝过绿茶 I haven't ever had green tea. 我学过弹钢琴。 I've learned playing the piano.
17	得	de	(助)	particle	读得好 / read well 说得不好 / speak not well 我学过弹钢琴,可是弹得不好。 I've learned playing the piano, but I'm not good at it.
18	经常	jīngcháng	(副)	often	经常喝茶 often drink tea 经常感冒 / always catch cold 我经常去商店。 I often go shopping.

13 我喜欢古典音乐
I Like Classical Music

| 19 | 每 | měi | （代） | every | 每天 / every day
每个星期 / every week
我每个星期六晚上都去听音乐会。/ I go to the concert every Saturday evening. |
| 20 | 同意 | tóngyì | （动） | to agree | 不同意 / don't agree
老师同意了。
The teacher agreed.
他同意星期六去参观美术馆。
He agreed on going to visit the art museum on Saturday. |

听力录音文本及参考答案
Recording Text and Answers

1. （1）女：你经常去听音乐会吧？
    男：是，每个星期六晚上都去。
   （2）男：你会弹钢琴吗？
    女：我学过一点儿，可是弹得不好。
   （3）女：星期六我们一起去听古典音乐会吧。
    男：我一点儿也不喜欢古典音乐，我喜欢流行音乐。
   （4）男：听音乐是一种享受。
    女：我同意。

    （1）√ （2）× （3）× （4）√

2. 略。
3. 略。
4. （4）—（2）—（3）—（5）—（1）
5. 略。

14 我代表公司欢迎您
Wǒ dàibiǎo gōngsī huānyíng nín
I Welcome You on Behalf of the Company

| 句型 | Sentence Patterns |

131. 请问，您是马丁先生吗？
Qǐng wèn, nín shì Mǎdīng xiānsheng ma?
Excuse me, are you Mr. Martin?

132. 我是中国中信公司的，我叫王大林。
Wǒ shì Zhōngguó Zhōngxìn Gōngsī de, wǒ jiào Wáng Dàlín.
I am from Zhongxin Company in China. I am Wang Dalin.

133. 我代表公司欢迎您。
Wǒ dàibiǎo gōngsī huānyíng nín.
I welcome you on behalf of my company.

134. 认识您很高兴。
Rènshi nín hěn gāoxìng.
It is nice to see you.

14 我代表公司欢迎您
I Welcome You on Behalf of the Company

135. 一路辛苦了！
Yí lù xīnkǔ le!

It must have been a tough trip!

136. 没什么。
Méi shénme.

No, not at all.

137. 您住长城饭店，可以吗？
Nín zhù Chángchéng Fàndiàn, kěyǐ ma?

Is it all right for you to stay at Great Wall Hotel?

138. 给您添麻烦了。
Gěi nín tiān máfan le.

Sorry to trouble you!

139. 我很满意。
Wǒ hěn mǎnyì.

I am very satisfied.

140. 不必客气。
Búbì kèqi.

You are welcome.

课文 | Text

（一）在机场接人 At the airport arrival hall

王大林： 请问，您是马丁先生吗？
Qǐngwèn, nín shì Mǎdīng xiānsheng ma?
Excuse me, are you Mr. Martin?

马　丁： 是，您是……？
Shì, nín shì…?
Yes, and you are...?

王大林： 我是中国中信公司的，我姓王。
Wǒ shì Zhōngguó Zhōngxìn Gōngsī de, wǒ xìng Wáng.
I am from Zhongxin Company in China. My surname is Wang.

马　丁： 王先生，您好。
Wáng xiānsheng, nín hǎo.
Mr. Wang, how do you do!

王大林： 您好，认识您很高兴。我代表公司欢迎您。
Nín hǎo, rènshi nín hěn gāoxìng. Wǒ dàibiǎo gōngsī huānyíng nín.
How do you do! I welcome you on behalf of my company.

马　丁： 认识您我也很高兴。
Rènshi nín wǒ yě hěn gāoxìng.
I am glad to see you too.

14 我代表公司欢迎您
I Welcome You on Behalf of the Company

王大林：一路辛苦了！
Yí lù xīnkǔ le!
It must have been a tough trip!

马　丁：没什么。
Méi shénme.
No, not at all.

(二) 在汽车里 In the car

马　丁：我们去哪儿？
Wǒmen qù nǎr?
Where are we going?

王大林：去饭店。
Qù fàndiàn.
To the hotel.

马　丁：去哪个饭店？
Qù nǎ ge fàndiàn?
To which hotel?

王大林：您住长城饭店，可以吗？
Nín zhù Chángchéng Fàndiàn, kěyǐ ma?
Is it all right for you to stay at Great Wall Hotel?

马　丁：很好，我很满意。给您添麻烦了。
Hěn hǎo, wǒ hěn mǎnyì. Gěi nín tiān máfan le.
I am very satisfied. Sorry to trouble you!

王大林：不必客气。
Búbì kèqi.
You are welcome.

（三）马丁先生来中国了 Mr. Martin has come to China

马丁 先生 来 中国 了。 中信 公司 的 王
Mǎdīng xiānsheng lái Zhōngguó le. Zhōngxìn Gōngsī de Wáng
先生 在飞机场 欢迎他。王 先生 说："马丁
xiānsheng zài fēijīchǎng huānyíng tā. Wáng xiānsheng shuō: "Mǎdīng
先生，一路上 辛苦了，我代表 公司 欢迎 您！"
xiānsheng, yílù shang xīnkǔ le, wǒ dàibiǎo gōngsī huānyíng nín."
马丁 先生 说："谢谢， 今天天气很好，路上
Mǎdīng xiānsheng shuō: " xièxie, jīntiān tiānqì hěn hǎo, lù shang
很 舒服。" 然后 他们要了出租车，一起 去了
hěn shūfu." Ránhòu tāmen yàole chūzūchē, yìqǐ qù le
长城 饭店。马丁 先生 要 住在那儿。
Chángchéng Fàndiàn. Mǎdīng xiānsheng yào zhù zài nàr.

Mr Martin has come to China. Mr Wang from Zhongxin Company was at the airport to meet him. Mr Wang said: "Mr. Martin, it must have been a tough trip. I welcome you I welcome you on behalf of my company!" Mr. Martin said: "Thank you. It's a good day and it has been a comfortable trip." Then they got a taxi to go to Great Wall Hotel together. Mr. Martin would stay there.

14 我代表公司欢迎您
I Welcome You on Behalf of the Company

注 释 | Annotation

1. 没什么。No, not at all.

   表示没关系、不介意。"没什么"也常用来回答别人的感谢。如：A："谢谢你。" B："没什么。"

   "没什么" indicates "It's all right" or "Do not mind". "没什么" is also often used to express gratitude to others, e.g. A: "谢谢你。" (Thank you.) B: "没什么。" (It is nothing.)

2. 给您添麻烦了。Sorry to trouble you.

   请人帮助后说的客气话，表示因打扰对方而道歉，并表示感谢。

   Formulae after asking for other people's help. It is used to express one's apology for troubling others and thanks for other's help.

语法 | Grammar

1. 住在那儿

"在+那儿"常用在动词后表示处所。也可以说"住在长城饭店""住在家里"。如：

"在+那儿" is often used after verbs to express location. For examples:

住在长城饭店

stay at Great Wall Hotel

住在家里

stay at home

2. 来、去

"来"和"去"都是动词，是以说话人为参照而言的。如：

"来" and "去" are both verbs. They are chosen according to the standpoint of the speaker. For examples:

马丁先生来中国了。（说话人在中国）

Mr. Martin has come to China. (The speaker is in China now.)

他们一起去了长城饭店。（说话人不在长城饭店）

They went to the Great Wall Hotel. (The speaker is not in the Great Wall Hotel now.)

14 我代表公司欢迎您
I Welcome You on Behalf of the Company

练习 | Exercises

1. 听录音,选择正确的回答:
Listen to the record and choose the correct answer:
(1)　a. 不谢!　　　　　b. 不客气!
　　　c. 没什么。　　　 d. 谢谢你!
(2)　a. 太好了!　　　　b. 很好!
　　　c. 不谢。　　　　 d. 不必客气!
(3)　a. 就在前边。　　　b. 不客气!
　　　c. 给您添麻烦了。　d. 不谢。

2. 连词成句:
Put the following words into sentences:
(1)　我　长城饭店　想　住　在
_____
(2)　欢迎　代表　公司　我　您
_____
(3)　很　认识　我　高兴　您　也
_____
(4)　麻烦　给　添　您　了
_____
(5)　我们　去　飞机场　一起　要
_____

3. 完成对话：

Complete the following dialogues:

(1) A：您是王大林先生吧？

B：是，＿＿＿＿＿＿＿＿＿＿

A：我代表公司欢迎您。

B：＿＿＿＿＿＿＿＿＿＿

A：认识您很高兴。

B：＿＿＿＿＿＿＿＿＿＿（也）

A：一路辛苦了。

B：＿＿＿＿＿＿＿＿＿＿

(2) A：我们去哪儿？

B：＿＿＿＿＿＿＿＿＿＿

A：饭店远不远？

B：不远，＿＿＿＿＿＿＿＿＿＿

A：谢谢您，给您添麻烦了。

B：＿＿＿＿＿＿＿＿＿＿

4. 把括号里的词放在合适的位置上：

Put the words in the brackets on the right place.

(1) 我a公司b欢迎您c。　　（代表）

(2) a您b很c高兴。　　（认识）

(3) a辛苦b了c！　　（一路）

(4) a您b添c麻烦了。　　（给）

(5) a我b满意c。　　（很）

(6) a必b客气c。　　（不）

14 我代表公司欢迎您
I Welcome You on Behalf of the Company

5. 用下列词语说一段话：

Make a speech with the following words:

题目：马丁先生来中国了

参考词语：来　去　辛苦　代表　欢迎　舒服　住

生词 | New Words

1	代表	dàibiǎo	（动）	to represent

他代表我们公司。
He represents our company.
他不代表我们公司。
He doesn't represent our company.
我代表公司欢迎你。
Here is my warm welcome on our company's behalf.

2	公司	gōngsī	（名）	company

一个公司 / a company
你现在去公司吗？
Are you going to the company now?
他代表我们公司。
He represents our company.

3	先生	xiānsheng	（名）	Mr, sir

王先生 / Mr. Wang
李先生 / Mr. Li
您好，先生！
Hello, sir!

4	认识	rènshi	（动）	to know

不认识 / don't know
我不认识他。
I don't know him.
你认识他吗？
Do you know him?

5	高兴	gāoxìng	（形）	glad

很高兴 / very glad
不高兴 / not happy
认识你很高兴。
Glad to know you.

6	一路上	yílù shang		all the way	一路上很高兴。 Very glad all the way. (一)路上很辛苦。 It's been a very tough trip! 一路上辛苦了。 It must have been a tough trip!
7	辛苦	xīnkǔ	（形）	tough	很辛苦 / very tiring 不辛苦 / not tiring 一路上辛苦了。 It must have been a tough trip!
8	没什么	méi shénme		nothing, not at all	没什么,不辛苦。 Not at all. It's not so tiring. 没什么,不用谢。 You are welcome. 没什么,别客气。 You are welcome.
9	给	gěi	（动）	to give	给你 / give it to you 给他 / give it to him 给你书。 Here is the book.
10	添	tiān	（动）	to give	添麻烦 / trouble someone 给你添麻烦了。 Sorry to trouble you! 我给他添了很多麻烦。 I troubled him much.
11	麻烦	máfan	（名）	trouble	有麻烦 / have some trouble 有很多麻烦。 have many troubles 给你添麻烦了。 Sorry to trouble you!
12	满意	mǎnyì	（形）	satisfy	很满意 / very satisfied 不满意 / not satisfied 我很满意。 I feel very satisfied.
13	不必	búbì	（副）	unnecessary, do not need to	不必说 / needless to say 不必去 / needless to go 你不必谢我。 You don't need to thank me.

14 我代表公司欢迎您
I Welcome You on Behalf of the Company

| 14 | 那儿 | nàr | （代） | there | 在那儿 / be there
去那儿 / go there
我要住在那儿。
I want to live there. |

专有名词：Proper nouns:

1	马丁	Mǎdīng	Martin
2	中国	Zhōngguó	China
3	中信公司	Zhōngxìn Gōngsī	Zhongxin Company
4	王大林	Wáng Dàlín	Wang Dalin, a Chinese name
5	长城	Chángchéng	Great Wall
6	长城饭店	Chángchéng Fàndiàn	Great Wall Hotel

听力录音文本及参考答案
Recording Text and Answers

1. （1）一路上辛苦了！
   （2）给您添麻烦了！
   （3）请问，长城饭店在哪儿？
   （1）c （2）d （3）a

2. （1）我想住在长城饭店。
   （2）我代表公司欢迎您。
   （3）认识您我也很高兴。/我也很高兴认识您。
   （4）给您添麻烦了。
   （5）我们要一起去飞机场。

3. 略。

4. （1）a （2）a （3）a （4）a （5）b （6）a

5. 略。

15 Wǒ xǐhuan xuéxí Zhōngwén
我喜欢学习中文
I Like Studying Chinese

句型 | Sentence Patterns

141. 你会说 中文 吗?
Nǐ huì shuō Zhōngwén ma?
Do you speak Chinese?

142. 你能看 中文 书吗?
Nǐ néng kàn Zhōngwén shū ma?
Can you read Chinese books?

143. 你为 什么要学习 中文?
Nǐ wèi shénme yào xuéxí Zhōngwén?
Why do you learn Chinese?

144. 中国 有几千年 的 历史。
Zhōngguó yǒu jǐ qiān nián de lìshǐ.
China has a history of several thousand years.

145. 我 想了解 中国。
Wǒ xiǎng liǎojiě Zhōngguó.
I want to find out more about China.

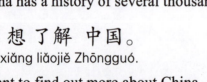

15 我喜欢学习中文
I Like Studying Chinese

146. 我 喜欢 中国 文学。
Wǒ xǐhuan Zhōngguó wénxué.

I like Chinese literature.

147. 我 要 努力 学习 中文，和 中国人 做 朋友。
Wǒ yào nǔlì xuéxí Zhōngwén, hé Zhōngguórén zuò péngyou.

I want to work hard to learn Chinese, and to make friends with Chinese people.

148. 我 打算 明年 去 中国 学习 汉语。
Wǒ dǎsuàn míngnián qù Zhōngguó xuéxí Hànyǔ.

I plan to go to China to study Chinese next year.

149. 我 说 中文，你 懂 不 懂？
Wǒ shuō Zhōngwén, nǐ dǒng bu dǒng?

I speak Chinese. Can you understand?

150. 请 慢一点儿 说。
Qǐng màn yìdiǎnr shuō.

Please speak slowly.

课文 | Text

(一)

女：你会说中文吗?
Nǐ huì shuō Zhōngwén ma?
Do you speak Chinese?

男：我会一点儿。
Wǒ huì yìdiǎnr.
I know a little.

女：你能看中文书吗?
Nǐ néng kàn Zhōngwénshū ma?
Can you read Chinese books?

男：还不能看。
Hái bù néng kàn.
I still cannot read (Chinese).

女：我说中文,你懂不懂?
Wǒ shuō Zhōngwén, nǐ dǒng bu dǒng?
I speak Chinese. Can you understand?

男：你慢一点儿说,我可以懂。
Nǐ màn yìdiǎnr shuō, wǒ kěyǐ dǒng.
If you speak slowly, I would understand.

15 我喜欢学习中文
I Like Studying Chinese

(二)

女：你学过 中文，是吗？
Nǐ xuéguo Zhōngwén, shì ma?
You have learnt Chinese, haven't you?

男：是，我学过 中文。
Shì, wǒ xuéguo Zhōngwén.
Yes, I have learnt Chinese.

女：你喜欢学习 中文 吗？
Nǐ xǐhuan xuéxí Zhōngwén ma?
Do you like studying Chinese?

男：是啊，我很喜欢学习中文。
Shì a, Wǒ hěn xǐhuan xuéxí Zhōngwén.
Yes, I like studying Chinese very much.

女：为 什么呢？
Wèi shénme ne?
Why?

男：因为我特别喜欢 中国 文学，我想 看 中文
Yīnwèi wǒ tèbié xǐhuan Zhōngguó wénxué, wǒ xiǎng kàn Zhōngwén
书，所以我来北京学习汉语了。
shū, suǒyǐ wǒ lái Běijīng xuéxí Hànyǔ le.
Because I like Chinese literature very much and I want to read Chinese books. So, I come to China to study Chinese.

（三）我要去中国 I want to go to China

中国 有几千年 的历史，我很 想 了解 中国。我 学过 中文，可是我的 中文 还不太 好，还不能 看 中文书。我打算 明年 去北京 学习汉语。我要努力学习中文，和 中国人 做 朋友。我还要 参观 博物馆、美术馆，还要 经常 去 听音乐会。我 很 喜欢 中国音乐。我也 很喜欢 中国 文学，我要看 中国 文学作品。

Zhōngguó yǒu jǐ qiān nián de lìshǐ, wǒ hěn xiǎng liǎojiě Zhōngguó. Wǒ xuéguo Zhōngwén, kěshì wǒ de Zhōngwén hái bú tài hǎo, hái bù néng kàn Zhōngwénshū. Wǒ dǎsuàn míngnián qù Běijīng xuéxí Hànyǔ. Wǒ yào nǔlì xuéxí Zhōngwén, hé Zhōngguórén zuò péngyou. Wǒ hái yào cānguān bówùguǎn, měishùguǎn, hái yào jīngcháng qù tīng yīnyuèhuì. Wǒ hěn xǐhuan Zhōngguó yīnyuè. Wǒ yě hěn xǐhuan Zhōngguó wénxué, wǒ yào kàn Zhōngguó wénxué zuòpǐn.

China has a history of several thousand years. I want to find out more about China. I have learnt Chinese. However, my Chinese is not good. I can not read Chinese books yet. I plan to go to Beijing to study Chinese next year. I will work hard to learn Chinese and make friends with Chinese people. I also want to visit the museums, art galleries, and I'll go to the concerts. I enjoy Chinese music very much. I also like Chinese literature. I want to read works of Chinese literature.

15 我喜欢学习中文
I Like Studying Chinese

注释 | Annotation

1. 是啊。Yes.

    "是啊"表示同意对方意见。

    "是啊" expresses one's agreement with the other party's opinions, and then a further explanation will be made.

2. 中国有几千年的历史。China has a history of several thousand years.

    中国的朝代从公元前21世纪开始,先后经历了夏、商、周、秦、汉、晋、南北朝、隋、唐、宋、辽、西夏、金、元、明、清等多个朝代。1949年10月1日中华人民共和国成立。

    China has a history of several thousand years. The dynasties that China goes through, starting from 2100 BC, are Xia, Shang, Zhou, Qin, Han, Jin, the Northern and Southern Dynasties, Sui, Tang, Song, Liao, the Western Xia, Jin, Yuan, Ming, and Qing. On Oct.1st, 1949, the People's Republic of China was founded.

语法 | Grammar

1. 能、会

"能"和"会"用在动词前面,表示能够做什么,具备什么能力。否定式为"不能""不会"。如:

"能" and "会" are used before verbs to express what man can manage to do and what capacities one possesses. The negative form is "不能","不会". For example:

我会弹钢琴。

I can play the piano.

他会说汉语。

He can speak Chinese.

我能看中文书了。

I come to be able to read Chinese book.

2. 为什么

询问原因,后面加动词,有时只加一个"呢",成为"为什么呢"。如:

"为什么" inquires about the reason and is followed by verbs. Sometimes only "呢" is added to form "为什么呢?" For example:

你为什么学习中文?

Why do you study Chinese?

你为什么不喜欢喝茶?

15 我喜欢学习中文
I Like Studying Chinese

Why do not you like drinking tea?

他说不想去听音乐会，为什么呢？

He said he didn't want to go to listen to the concert, why?

练习 | Exercises

1. 听录音，判断对错：

Listen to the record and judge whether the following statements are right or not:

(1) 女的不能看中文书。 ☐
(2) 男的学过中文。 ☐
(3) 女的很喜欢中国音乐。 ☐
(4) 大卫要去参观美术馆。 ☐

2. 完成句子：

Complete the following sentences:

(1) A：你会说中文吗？
　　B：不，_____
　　A：你想学习中文吗？
　　B：是的，_____
　　A：你为什么想学习中文？
　　B：_____

(2) A：你喜欢中国文学吗？
　　B：是的，_____
　　A：你能看中国文学作品吗？
　　B：不，_____
　　A：你能说中文吗？
　　B：_____
(3) A：我说中文，你懂不懂？
　　B：_____（慢一点儿）
　　A：你学过中文吗？
　　B：是的，_____（学过一点儿）
(4) A：你打算去中国，是吗？
　　B：是的，_____
　　A：去干什么？
　　B：_____
　　A：你打算去中国哪儿？
　　B：_____

3. 翻译词组：

Translation:
(1) 了解中国　　　　　　了解中国文学
　　了解中国历史　　　　了解中国公司
(2) 为什么要去中国　　　为什么要参观美术馆
　　为什么学习中文　　　为什么不喜欢喝咖啡
(3) 会说中文　　　　　　会弹钢琴
　　能看中文书　　　　　能听懂中文

15 我喜欢学习中文
I Like Studying Chinese

(4) 打算休息休息　　　打算去参观博物馆
　　打算听听音乐　　　打算去商店

4. 选词填空：

Fill in the following blanks with proper word:

历史　了解　正在　现在　能　还　打算　喜欢
博物馆　听音乐　做朋友

我叫大卫。我（　　）学习中文。中国有几千年的（　　），我很想（　　）中国。（　　）我的中文（　　）不太好，还不（　　）看中文书。我（　　）去北京学习汉语。我要和中国人（　　），我还要参观（　　），还要经常（　　），我很（　　）中国音乐。

5. 用下列词语说一段话：

Make a speech with the following words

题目：我为什么学习汉语

参考词语：因为　所以　了解　中国　历史　文学　努力

生词 | New Words

1	能	néng	（动）	can	能说中文 can speak Chinese 能看中文书 can read Chinese books 你能弹钢琴吗？ Can you play the piano?
2	为什么	wèi shénme		why	他为什么不去上课？ Why didn't he attend class? 你为什么不喝绿茶？ Why don't you drink green tea? 你们为什么不一起去听音乐会？ Why not go to the concert together?
3	学习	xuéxí	（动）	to learn	学习生词 / learn new words 学习弹钢琴 learn playing the piano 他在家学习呢。 He is studying at home.
4	千	qiān	（数）	thousand	一千 / one thousand 五千 / five thousand 几千个人 thousands of people
5	年	nián	（名）	year	几千年 / thousands of years 2015年 / year 2015 我学习中文一年了。 I have studied Chinese for one year.
6	历史	lìshǐ	（名）	history	中国历史 Chinese history 三千年的历史 a history of three thousand years 中国有几千年的历史。 China has a history of several thousand years.

15 我喜欢学习中文
I Like Studying Chinese

7	了解	liǎojiě	(动)	to understand	特别了解 understand very well 了解古典音乐 understand classical music 我还不太了解中国。 I still don't know much about China.
8	文学	wénxué	(名)	literature	文学作品 works of literature 古典文学 classical literature 我喜欢中国文学。 I love Chinese literature.
9	努力	nǔlì	(形)	work hard	很努力 / with great efforts 努力学习 / study hard 他学习很努力。 He studies very hard.
10	明年	míngnián	(名)	next year	明年去中国 go to China next year 明年我要学习弹钢琴。 I want to learn playing piano next year. 明年你打算做什么？ What's your plan for the next year?
11	懂	dǒng	(动)	to understand	听懂了 / understand 看不懂 / be blind to 我说汉语你懂不懂？ Do you understand me if I speak Chinese?
12	慢	màn	(形)	slow	太慢了 / too slow 慢一点儿 slow it down a little 请慢一点儿说。 Could you please slow it down a little?

13	因为	yīnwèi	（介）	because	因为风太大了，我们不去参观博物馆了。 We don't go to visit the museum because of the big wind. 因为没有咖啡，他喝了一杯红茶。 He had a cup of red tea because there's no coffee. 因为我没听懂，所以请再说一遍。 I didn't catch you, so could you please say it again?
14	所以	suǒyǐ	（连）	so, therefore	我喜欢中国，所以我学习汉语了。 I love China, so I choose to study Chinese. 我看了几本中国历史书，所以我了解了一点儿中国历史。 I've read several books about Chinese history, so I know a little about the history of China. 我喜欢音乐，所以我每个星期六都去听音乐会。 I love music, so I go to the concert every Saturday.
15	来	lái	（动）	to come	来北京 / come to Beijing 来中国 / come to China 你几点来我家？ When will you come to my house?
16	作品	zuòpǐn	（名）	works	文学作品 / works of literature 音乐作品 / musical works 你看过中国的文学作品吗？ Have you read any works of Chinese literature?
17	美术馆	měishù guǎn	（名）	art museum	参观美术馆 visit the art museum 一起去美术馆吧？ Let go to the art museum together? 请问，去美术馆怎么走？ Excuse me, how can I get to the art museum?

15 我喜欢学习中文
I Like Studying Chinese

专有名词：Proper nouns:

1	中文	Zhōngwén	Chinese language
2	中国人	Zhōngguórén	Chinese, Chinese people
3	北京	Běijīng	Beijing, capital of China
4	汉语	Hànyǔ	Chinese

听力录音文本及参考答案
Recording Text and Answers

1. (1) 男：你能看中文书吗？
    女：我能看一点儿。
   (2) 女：你学过中文，是吗？
    男：是，我学过一年中文。
   (3) 男：你为什么学习中文？
    女：中国有几千年的历史，我很想了解中国。
   (4) 女：大卫，一起去参观美术馆吧？
    男：我现在没空儿，不能去。

   (1) × (2) √ (3) × (4) ×

2. 略。

3. 略。

4. 正在　　　历史
   了解　　　现在
   还　　　　能
   打算　　　做朋友
   博物馆　　听音乐　　喜欢

5. 略。

生词总表
Vocabulary

	A	
爱	ài	13

	B	
吧	ba	7
拜访	bàifǎng	7
半	bàn	2
杯	bēi	11
本	běn	12
比较	bǐjiào	13
遍	biàn	3
别的	biéde	8
病	bìng	10
博物馆	bówùguǎn	12
不	bù	3
不必	búbì	14
不错	búcuò	10
不用(谢)	búyòng (xiè)	4

	C	
参观	cānguān	12
茶	chá	11
差	chà	2
车	chē	5
出去	chūqù	12
出租车	chūzūchē	5
次	cì	3

	D	
打开	dǎkāi	3
打算	dǎsuàn	12
大	dà	9
代表	dàibiǎo	14
单	dān	6
淡	dàn	11
到	dào	5
的	de	6
得	de	13
登记表	dēngjìbiǎo	6
等	děng	5
地方	dìfang	5
点	diǎn	2
懂	dǒng	15
都	dōu	1
读	dú	3
肚子	dùzi	10
对	duì	7

生词总表 Vocabulary

对不起	duìbuqǐ	5		喝	hē	11
多少	duōshao	8		合适	héshì	7
				和	hé	7
F				盒	hé	8
饭店	fàndiàn	5		很	hěn	1
房间	fángjiān	6		红	hóng	11
房卡	fángkǎ	6		花茶	huāchá	11
分	fēn	2		欢迎	huānyíng	7
风	fēng	9		会	huì	13
G				**J**		
感冒	gǎnmào	10		极	jí	9
干	gàn	12		几	jǐ	2
钢琴	gāngqín	13		加	jiā	11
高兴	gāoxìng	14		家	jiā	7
个	gè	8		间	jiān	6
给	gěi	14		健康	jiànkāng	10
跟	gēn	6		叫	jiào	1
公司	gōngsī	14		今天	jīntiān	2
古典	gǔdiǎn	13		经常	jīngcháng	13
刮	guā	9		就	jiù	5
拐	guǎi	4		橘子	júzi	8
贵	guì	8				
过	guo	13		**K**		
				咖啡	kāfēi	11
H				开	kāi	2
还	hái	8		看	kàn	9
还是	háishi	6		可以	kěyǐ	7
好	hǎo	1		刻	kè	2
号	hào	6		客气	kèqi	4

课文	kèwén	3		门	mén	2
空	kōng	6		面包	miànbāo	8
空儿	kòngr	7		明白	míngbai	3
块(元)	kuài (yuán)	8		明年	míngnián	15

	L				N	
来	lái	15		哪	nǎ	13
老师	lǎoshī	3		哪儿	nǎr	4
冷	lěng	9		那	nà	11
历史	lìshǐ	15		那儿	nàr	14
练习	liànxí	3		呢	ne	1
两	liǎng	6		能	néng	15
了	le	2		你	nǐ	1
了解	liǎojiě	15		你们	nǐmen	1
流行	liúxíng	13		年	nián	15
绿	lǜ	11		您	nín	1
				牛奶	niúnǎi	8
				浓	nóng	11
	M			努力	nǔlì	15
麻烦	máfan	14				
马路	mǎlù	4			P	
吗	ma	1				
买	mǎi	8		旁边	pángbiān	4
满	mǎn	6		朋友	péngyou	12
满意	mǎnyì	14		啤酒	píjiǔ	11
慢	màn	15		便宜	piányi	8
毛(角)	máo (jiǎo)	8		苹果	píngguǒ	8
没什么	méi shénme	14				
没有	méiyǒu	5			Q	
每	měi	13		千	qiān	15
美术馆	měishùguǎn	15		前边	qiánbian	4

生词总表 Vocabulary

钱	qián	8
晴天	qíngtiān	9
请	qǐng	3
曲	qǔ	13
去	qù	5

R

然后	ránhòu	12
热	rè	9
人	rén	6
认识	rènshi	14

S

商店	shāngdiàn	2
上	shàng	5
上课	shàng kè	3
身体	shēntǐ	10
生词	shēngcí	3
什么	shénme	1
时间	shíjiān	7
事	shì	7
试	shì	11
是	shì	2
书	shū	3
舒服	shūfu	10
双	shuāng	6
说	shuō	3
所以	suǒyǐ	15

T

他	tā	1
她	tā	6
他们	tāmen	7
太	tài	8
弹	tán	13
糖	táng	11
特别	tèbié	9
疼	téng	10
天气	tiānqì	9
添	tiān	14
甜	tián	11
填	tián	6
听	tīng	13
同学们	tóngxuémen	3
同意	tóngyì	13
头	tóu	10

W

外面	wàimiàn	9
晚上	wǎnshang	7
往	wǎng	4
为什么	wèi shénme	15
位	wèi	12
文学	wénxué	15
问	wèn	4
我	wǒ	1
我们	wǒmen	1

X

喜欢	xǐhuan	11
下(雨)	xià(yǔ)	9
下课	xià kè	3

下午	xiàwǔ	7		阴天	yīntiān	9
先	xiān	12		音乐	yīnyuè	13
先生	xiānsheng	14		银行	yínháng	2
现在	xiànzài	2		应该	yīnggāi	10
香	xiāng	11		有	yǒu	5
享受	xiǎngshòu	13		有点儿	yǒudiǎnr	10
想	xiǎng	7		有意思	yǒu yìsi	12
谢谢	xièxie	4		右	yòu	4
辛苦	xīnkǔ	14		右边	yòubian	4
星期	xīngqī	2		远	yuǎn	4
星期日(天)	xīngqīrì	2				
行	xíng	7		**Z**		
休息	xiūxi	10		再	zài	3
需要	xūyào	10		再见	zàijiàn	7
学	xué	13		在	zài	4/12
学习	xuéxí	15		怎么	zěnme	4
				怎么样	zěnmeyàng	9
Y				这	zhè	6
要	yào	5/9		正在	zhèngzài	12
也	yě	1		知道	zhīdao	11
一点儿	yìdiǎnr	8		种	zhǒng	13
一共	yígòng	8		住	zhù	6
一会儿	yíhuìr	5		走	zǒu	4
一路上	yílù shang	14		最	zuì	13
一起	yìqǐ	7		左	zuǒ	4
一下儿	yíxiàr	8		左边	zuǒbian	4
医院	yīyuàn	10		作品	zuòpǐn	15
意思	yìsi	12		做	zuò	3
因为	yīnwèi	15				

专有名词
Proper Nouns

	B	
北京	Běijīng	15
北京饭店	Běijīng Fàndiàn	5
	C	
长城	Chángchéng	14
长城饭店	Chángchéng Fàndiàn	14
	D	
大卫	Dàwèi	1
	H	
汉语	Hànyǔ	15

	M	
马丁	Mǎdīng	14
	W	
王大林	Wáng Dàlín	14
王红	Wáng Hóng	1
王明	Wáng Míng	1
	Z	
中国	Zhōngguó	14
中国人	Zhōngguórén	15
中文	Zhōngwén	15
中信公司	Zhōngxìn Gōngsī	14

附录一
Appendix I

Yǔfǎ Shùyǔ Jiǎnchēng Biǎo
语法术语简称表
The Abbreviations of Chinese Grammatical Terms

名词	（名）	míngcí	noun
代词	（代）	dàicí	pronoun
动词	（动）	dòngcí	verb
助动词	（助动）	zhùdòngcí	auxiliary verb
形容词	（形）	xíngróngcí	adjective
数词	（数）	shùcí	numeral
量词	（量）	liàngcí	measure word
副词	（副）	fùcí	adverb
介词	（介）	jiècí	preposition
连词	（连）	liáncí	conjunction
助词	（助）	zhùcí	auxiliary word
叹词	（叹）	tàncí	interjection
拟声词	（拟声）	nǐshēngcí	mimetic word
词头	（头）	cítóu	prefix
词尾	（尾）	cíwěi	suffix
主语	（主）	zhǔyǔ	subject
谓语	（谓）	wèiyǔ	predicate
宾语	（宾）	bīnyǔ	object
定语	（定）	dìngyǔ	attribute
状语	（状）	zhuàngyǔ	adverbial
补语	（补）	bǔyǔ	complement

附录二
Appendix II

Hànyǔ Yǔyīn
汉语语音
Chinese Pronunciation

音节是现代汉语的语音单位，一个音节往往就是一个词，并且对应一个汉字。汉语的音节通常由三部分组成：声母、韵母和声调。例如：mā, m 是声母，a 是韵母，- 是声调。

In modern Chinese a syllable constitutes a phonetic unit and usually stands as a word with the meaning expressed by a Chinese character. A Chinese syllable is composed of three parts: an initial, a final and a tone. Take mā for example. m is the initial, a is the final, - is the tone and the meaning is expressed by the character "妈" (mother).

一、声母　The Initials

b	p	m	f		d	t	n	l
g	k	h			j	q	x	
zh	ch	sh	r		z	c	s	

汉语有21个声母，其中有12个声母在英语中有大致相同的音，它们是：
There are 21 initials in Chinese and 12 of them have almost the same pronunciation as in English:

1. 唇音 labial

b [p]　　　　　like the p in spy (not like the b in bay)

p [pʻ]　　　　like the p in pay

m [m]　　　　like the m in may

f [f]　　　　　like the f in fact

2. 舌尖前音 blade-alveolar

s [s]　　　　　like the s in say

3. 舌尖中音 alveolar

d [t]　　　　　like the t in stay

t [t']　　　　 like the t in tea

n [n]　　　　　like the n in name

l [l]　　　　　like the l in lay

4. 舌根音 velar

g [k]　　　　　like the k in sky (not like the g in guy)

k [k']　　　　 like the k in king

h [h]　　　　　like the h in high

方括号[]里是国际音标。

The International Phonetic Alphabets are in the brackets.

其余的9个，英语中只有近似音，它们是：

The other 9 only have similar pronunciation to that of English:

5. 舌尖前音 z、c blade-alveolar z, c

发音时，用舌尖接触上牙齿背，舌位和发s时相同，如图：

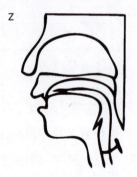

When pronouncing, put the tip of the tongue against the back of the upper teeth and the tongue position is the same as that of s, as is shown in the chart above:

6. 舌尖后音 zh、ch、sh、r   blade-palatal zh, ch, sh, r

发音时，舌头在口腔里的位置比发 z、c 时稍后一点，舌尖翘起接触硬腭最前端。如图：

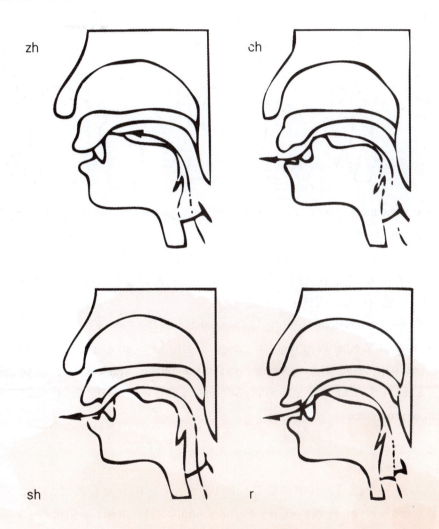

When pronouncing, keep the position of the tongue in the oral cavity, a little more backward than that of z or c, with the tip of tongue turned up against the foremost part of the hard palate. See the chart:

7. 舌面音 j、q、x   palatal j, q, x

发音时用舌面前部接触硬腭前部。如图：

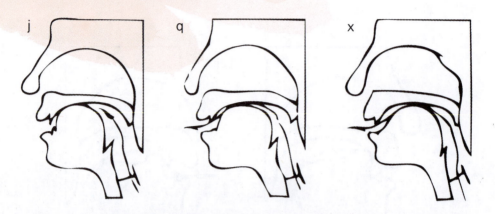

When pronouncing, raise the front part of your tongue against the front part of your hard palate, as is shown in the chart:

注意：英语 chew、cheap、shoe 中 ch[tʃ]不送气)，ch[tʃ']（送气），sh[ʃ]音介乎 zh、ch、和 j、q、x 二者之间。发[tʃ][tʃ']时要用舌面最前端、靠近舌尖的地方接触硬腭，往前一点儿，发成 j、q、x。

Note: ch[tʃ] (unaspirated), ch[tʃ'] (aspirated), sh[ʃ]in "chew"," cheap" and "shoe" in English are between the two groups of zh、ch、sh and j、q、x. When pronouncing [tʃ][tʃ']and [ʃ],the foremost part of the tongue, which is near the tip, is against the hard palate, and the tongue is positioned a little more to the front, thus j、q and x can be pronounced.

二、韵母　The Finals

汉语共有36个韵母。其中单韵母6个（a, o, e, i, u, ü），复合韵母29个，其中9个是基础韵母（ai, ei, ao, ou, an, en, ang, eng, ong），由6个单韵母和9个基础韵母拼合出其余的韵母。如下表：

There are 36 finals in Chinese. 6 of them are simple finals (a, o, e, i, u, ü), the other 29 are compound finals, among which 9 are basic finals (ai, ei, ao, ou, an, en,

ang, eng, ong). The 6 simple finals combine with the 9 basic finals to make up the other twenty finals, as is shown in the following table:

	i	u	ü
a	ia	ua	
o		uo	
e	ie		üe
ai		uai	
ei		uei	
ao	iao		
ou	iou		
an	ian	uan	üan
en	ien	uen	üen
ang	iang	uang	
eng	ieng	ueng	
ong	iong		

此外，还有一个不与声母拼合的韵母 er。
There is a final er, which cannot be combined with initials.

三、声调 The Tones

在汉语里，音节的高低升降能区别意义，例如：mǎi（买），mài（卖）。汉语的声调有四个，分别用 ˉ ˊ ˇ ˋ 来表示。

In Chinese the variation of a syllable's pitch may distinguish the meanings, e.g. mǎi (to buy) and mài (to sell). There are four tones in Chinese, and they are expressed respectively by ˉ ˊ ˇ ˋ.

第一声	the first tone	高调	the high tone
第二声	the second tone	升调	the rising tone
第三声	the third tone	低调	the low tone

| 第四声 | the fourth tone | 降调 | the falling tone |

例如： e.g.

mā	妈	mother
má	麻	hemp
mǎ	马	horse
mà	骂	scold

说明：

1. 音节 zhi, chi, shi, ri, zi, ci, si 中的韵母 i 不发 [i] 音。
2. 以 i 和 u 开头的音节，要分别改为 y、w，例如 iao→yao, ua→wa

   i、in、ing、u 自成音节时，写成 yi、yin、ying、wu。
3. ü 自成音节写成 yu。

   以 ü 开头的音节写成 yue、yuan、yun，两点省略。

   jü、qü、xü 写成 ju、qu、xu，两点也省略。
4. iou、uei、uen 前面有声母时，写作 iu、ui、un。

Clarifications:

1. The final i in syllables such as zhi, chi, shi, ri, zi, ci and si is silent and should not be pronounced as [i].
2. When a syllable starts with i or u, they should be changed into y and w respectively, e.g. iao→yao, ua→wa

   When i, in, ing and u form syllables by themselves, they are written respectively as yi, yin, ying and wu.
3. When ü forms a syllable by itself, it is written as yu. When syllables start with ü, they are written as yue、yuan and yun. The two dots are omitted.

   jü, qü, xü are written as ju, qu, xu, and the two dots are also omitted.
4. When preceded by initials, iou, uei and uen are written respectively as iu, ui and un.

附录三
Appendix III

Chángyòng Fǎnyì Dānyīnjié Xíngróngcí
常用反义单音节形容词
Some Useful Antonymous Adjectives with Single Syllable

大——小	多——少	远——近	高——低
dà xiǎo	duō shǎo	yuǎn jìn	gāo dī
big small	many few	far near	high low

先——后	早——晚	长——短	深——浅
xiān hòu	zǎo wǎn	cháng duǎn	shēn qiǎn
before after	early late	long short	deep shallow

真——假	冷——热	宽——窄	粗——细
zhēn jiǎ	lěng rè	kuān zhǎi	cū xì
true false	cold hot	broad narrow	thick thin

香——臭	浓——淡	强——弱	软——硬
xiāng chòu	nóng dàn	qiáng ruò	ruǎn yìng
fragrant stink	thick light	strong weak	soft hard

快——慢	薄——厚	胖——瘦	轻——重
kuài màn	báo hòu	pàng shòu	qīng zhòng
quick slow	thin thick	fat thin	light heavy

干——湿	穷——富	忙——闲	美——丑
gān shī	qióng fù	máng xián	měi chǒu
dry wet	poor rich	busy free	beautiful ugly

附录四
Appendix IV

Chángyòng Súyǔ

常用俗语

Some Useful Proverbs

1. 一年之计在于春，一天之计在于晨。
   Yì nián zhī jì zàiyú chūn, yì tiān zhī jì záiyú chén.
   The whole year's work depends on a good start in the Spring; a whole day's work depends on a good start in the morning.

2. 天下无难事，只怕有心人。
   Tiānxià wú nánshì, zhǐ pà yǒuxīn rén.
   Where there is a will, there is a way.

3. 不怕慢，就怕站。
   Bú pà màn, jiù pà zhàn.
   It is better to move slowly than stop.

4. 活到老，学到老。
   Huó dào lǎo, xué dào lǎo.
   A day I live, a day I study.

5. 种瓜得瓜，种豆得豆。
   Zhòng guā dé guā, zhòng dòu dé dòu.
   You harvest what you plant (sow).

6. 名师出高徒。
   Míng shī chū gāo tú.
   A good teacher will turn out good students.

7. 一个巴掌拍不响。
   Yí ge bāzhang pāi bù xiǎng.
   One person alone can not start a quarrel.(one hand only can not make an applause.)

Appendix IV

8. 在家靠父母，出门靠朋友。

   Zài jiā kào fùmǔ, chū mén kào péngyou.

   While at home we can turn to our parents, in our trip, to our friends.

9. 知足者长乐。

   Zhī zú zhě cháng lè.

   Satisfaction makes pleasure.

10. 好事不出门，坏事传千里。

    Hǎo shì bù chū mén, huài shì chuán qiān lǐ.

    Bad news travels far.

附录五
Appendix V

Gǔ Shī Sì Shǒu
古诗四首
Four Ancient Poems

唐 代（Tang Dynasty）
Táng Dài

李 白（701—762）
Lǐ Bái

静 夜 思
jìng yè sī

床　前　明　月　光，
chuáng qián míng yuè guāng

疑　是　地　上　霜。
yí shì dì shàng shuāng

举　头　望　明　月，
jǔ tóu wàng míng yuè

低　头　思　故　乡。
dī tóu sī gù xiāng

A TRANQUIL NIGHT

Before my bed a pool of light;
Can it be hoarfrost on the ground?
Looking up, I find the moon bright;
Bowing, in homesickness I'm drowned.

附录五 Appendix V

唐 代（Tang Dynasty）
Táng Dài

孟 浩 然（689—740）
Mèng Hàorán

春 晓
chūn xiǎo

春 眠 不 觉 晓，
chūn mián bù jué xiǎo

处 处 闻 啼 鸟。
chù chù wén tí niǎo

夜 来 风 雨 声，
yè lái fēng yǔ shēng

花 落 知 多 少。
huā luò zhī duō shǎo

SPRING MORNING

Spring morning in bed I'm lying,
Not to awake till birds are crying.
After one night of wind and showers,
How many are the fallen flowers?

唐 代（Tang Dynasty）
Táng Dài

王 之 涣（688—742）
Wáng Zhīhuàn

登 鹳 雀 楼
dēng guàn què lóu

白 日 依 山 尽，
bái rì yī shān jìn

黄 河 入 海 流。
huáng hé rù hǎi liú

欲 穷 千 里 目，
yù qióng qiān lǐ mù

更 上 一 层 楼。
gèng shàng yì céng lóu

THE STORK TOWER

The sun beyond the mountain glows;
The Yellow River seawards flows.
You can enjoy a grander sight
By climbing to a greater height.